Brilliant Stories for Assemblies

Paul Urry

Brilliant
PUBLICATIONS

To Eleanor

Published by
Brilliant Publications
Unit 10,
Sparrow Hall Farm,
Edlesborough,
Dunstable,
Bedfordshire
LU6 2ES, UK

Sales and stock enquiries:
Tel: 01202 712910
Fax: 0845 1309300
E-mail: brilliant@bebc.co.uk
Website: www.brilliantpublications.co.uk
General information enquiries:
Tel: 01525 222292

The name 'Brilliant Publications' and the logo are
registered trademarks.

First printed and published in the UK in 2004.
Reprinted in the UK in 2005, 2007 and 2009.
10 9 8 7 6 5 4

Written by Paul Urry
Illustrated by Val Edgar
Front cover illustration by Debbie Clark, Beehive
Illustration

© Paul Urry 2004
ISBN 978 1 903853 49 8

Contents

Introduction

Interactive stories are a powerful and immediate way of conveying emotions, situations and information.

The stories in this book allow the teller to read, refine or adapt a variety of tales for a particular situation or audience. The collection covers a wide range of themes. Different stories can be used at specific times of the year, when issues arise or just when you are suddenly called upon to do an assembly! Many of them can also be adapted for class assemblies or different key stages.

The book is divided into four chapters:

Cultural stories

The cultural story section explores a wide variety of experiences from around the world. It includes tales that explain the world around us, folklore and fantasy characters.

Religious stories

Stories from the six main world faiths are retold in the religious section. The focus of these is on the main figures in each religion, their acts, words and decisions.

Moral stories

Children are at the centre of the moral section. Each story looks at a different situation, allowing the listeners to imagine themselves in the place of the characters and to reflect on how they would react in a similar situation.

Historical stories

The historical stories in this book explore the facts and examine the actions taken by individuals and focus on the outcome of events. Each of the main historical periods of the Key Stage 2 curriculum are explored in the historical section. The stories include accurate retellings, myths and factual-based fiction.

Each story ends with suggested questions to explore with the audience. These can be refined into prayers.

For some stories props are suggested. These can be obtained from resources within school, the Internet or books. The list of Useful websites (page 94–95) provides background information for almost all the cultural, religious and historical stories. Many of the websites contain photographs and illustrations that can be downloaded. The illustrations on the sheets themselves can be enlarged and photocopied.

How people got fire
(Native American story)

: **Props suggested**
- Pictures of the animals involved:
- fireflies, fox, geese, hawk.

Note: This story can be acted out with face masks.

Native Americans looked at the world around them. They saw the stars, the animals and the plants and created stories about all of them. They did not write the stories down at first, but told them to the children. As the children got older they remembered the stories and told them to their children. The stories are usually set long before people arrived on the earth. This one is about the dangers of fire and how people got it.

A long time ago, when all the animals lived happily together, all the fire in the world stayed in one place with the fireflies.

Fox wanted to learn to fly like his friend Goose. Goose thought for a while about this and eventually said the geese would help him, but he must not open his eyes when they were flying. Fox agreed and they put some wings on him.

Fox was greedy and selfish. Although the geese had helped him fly and he enjoyed the feeling of moving through the air he was still not happy with this extra gift. He wanted more.

On one occasion when Fox and Goose were flying together it suddenly got warm as they flew over the walled village of the fireflies. Forgetting what Goose had said, Fox opened his eyes to see what it was. Immediately, his wings disappeared and he fell to the ground with a large thud.

Two fireflies came to see how Fox was. He asked how he could escape from the village as there was a large wall all the way round to stop the fire getting out.

The fireflies said that a tree would bend down and lift him out; all he had to do was ask. The nice fireflies asked him to stay for a while to look around the village.

In the centre of the village was a large fire. Fox saw how warm it was and wanted some for himself. He carefully snapped off a small branch and tied it to his tail. As he spoke to the fireflies he placed the branch in the fire. Slowly it caught light. As soon as Fox saw this he started running for the tree to get him out. 'Help me out!' he shouted to the tree. With the fireflies chasing Fox, the tree bent down and took him out of the village. Everywhere Fox ran, the branch kept touching plants, which caught fire. He threw it off his tail and gave it to Hawk. As Hawk carried it away sparks fell to earth and spread the fire.

Fox ran down his hole and hid from the other animals, knowing that he had damaged the earth.

Follow-up questions
- Why do you think Fox did this?
- How do you think the fireflies felt?

Brilliant Stories for Assemblies
© Paul Urry

This page may be photocopied by the purchasing institution only.

5

The greedy fisherman
(Aboriginal story)

In Aboriginal stories, there are lots of animals and gods. The Aborigines looked at the world around them and made up stories to explain why things are the way they are. Here is one story about a special type of fish and how not to be greedy!

Two men went to the river to catch some fish for their village. They untied their canoe from the bank and slowly paddled their way out into the middle of the river. There, they put the paddles in the boat and carefully threw their nets into the water. The men expected to stay there all day and collect only a few fish, but quickly their nets filled up.

The men hauled the nets into the canoe and emptied out the fish. They could not believe their eyes! So they threw the net back into the water. Again they filled with fish. They continued to collect fish until their canoe was full. The men were very pleased with themselves. 'Imagine what the people in the village are going to say when they see what a great quantity of food we have,' one said to the other.

As they paddled the canoe back to the bank they noticed a strange man walking towards them. They looked at each other and decided that they were not going to share any of their fish with him so they covered the great catch.

As they got to the bank the man called out, 'Hello friends! I am hungry and have no food. Do you have a couple of fish to spare?'

The men looked at each other. 'No,' they lied,' we only have enough for our village.'

The man stood there and then began to walk away. As he went into the distance he turned around and shouted, 'You have lied to me! Now no one will be able to enjoy the fish!'

The men did not understand what he had said, but they took the fish back to the village. They started to cut the fish but saw that the bones in them were very small. 'If we try to eat these we will choke on the bones and there are too many to take out. We cannot eat any of these.'

They told the older people in the village what had happened.

'Fools!' they said. 'Why didn't you share your fish? Didn't you realize that that was not any man but a great spirit? Because of your greed no one can eat these fish again.'

The men realized how selfish they had been but it was too late.

Follow-up question
◆ Can you think of anything you have, or a particular skill, that you could share with your family or friends?

Brilliant Stories for Assemblies
© Paul Urry

Beddgelert
(North Wales)

Note: You could look at how the story might be a 19th century creation for tourist purposes!

Seven hundred years ago great princes ruled different parts of North Wales. One of the greatest was called Llewelyn. He had a favourite hunting dog called Gelert. They were always together. One day, however, Llewelyn heard that a wolf was in the area. He told Gelert to stay behind to protect his son whilst he went hunting. Gelert wanted to go but knew how important Llewelyn's son was to him.

As he watched his master disappear out of the castle on his horse, Gelert went to where the child was asleep and lay on the floor next to him.

After a while, he woke up hearing a sound on the castle stairs. Gelert used his good sense of smell. This was no person. He could smell a wolf. Quickly and carefully he picked the child up, hid him behind a curtain and watched the door. Slowly it opened. He saw the snout of the wolf, smelling the air. It knew that there was food in the room. The wolf crept in. With a giant leap Gelert jumped onto the wolf. There was a great struggle; claws were digging into each other, teeth were ripping out fur, blood began to spill onto the floor. They banged into the cot and the sheet rolled around on the floor, mixing with the blood and dirt already there.

Finally Gelert raised his body high into the air and bit deep into the neck of the wolf. With a yelp the wolf fell to the ground, dead.

Exhausted, Gelert collapsed.

Later that day Llewelyn returned home. He called for Gelert but he did not come running. Llewelyn was surprised and ran up to his son's room. As he entered all he saw was Gelert on the floor with his teeth and claws dripping in blood. He looked at the cot – it was empty! Thinking Gelert had killed his son, he took his sword from his belt and plunged it deep into the chest of Gelert. As the dog let out a dying yelp, Llewelyn heard a cry from behind a curtain. He walked over and saw his son unharmed on the floor. Looking around the devastation of the room he saw the dead wolf. He quickly realized what had happened and cried out, 'What have I done?'

He carried the body of his faithful friend down to their favourite place by the river. There he buried Gelert under a tree and named the place Beddgelert – the grave of Gelert, so that all who pass through would know that Gelert was the faithful dog of Prince Llewelyn.

Follow-up question

It is important not to act quickly but to think before you do or say things.

◆ Can you think of a time you did something without thinking and later regretted it?

Brilliant Stories for Assemblies
© Paul Urry

This page may be photocopied by the purchasing institution only.

7

The bear in the quicksand
(Ancient Greek fable)

The Ancient Greeks told many stories about people. To make the stories more interesting and help people remember them they had animals in place of humans. These animals could talk. Some of them were clever animals, others did silly things – just like people. Here is one story about an animal that needed help and what the other animals did about it.

One day a bear was walking quietly on the sand. Suddenly he felt a funny feeling in his feet. He looked down and realized that he was sinking – quicksand, he thought, and tried to lift his feet out, but the more he tried, the deeper he sank into the sand. He looked around for help. In the distance he saw a monkey.

'Monkey, please help me. I am sinking into the sand!'

'I don't know if I should help you,' Monkey said. 'It is your own fault that you are in there. You should have known there was quicksand there.' The monkey was still criticising the bear when an owl arrived to find out what all the noise was.

'Please help me out of the quicksand,' pleaded the bear.

'Oh dear,' said the owl, 'I cannot save you. Nobody can save you. You should just accept that you are slowly going to sink into the sand. That is what I would do. Just wait.'

As the bear sank deeper into the sand a beaver appeared. 'What's going on here?' she asked.

'Please!' begged the bear. 'Won't someone help me get out of the sand?' Straight away the beaver ran up a tree. She ate quickly through some vines and dragged them to the side of the quicksand. She then called to the bear.

'Tie these together, then throw one end back to me.' The bear did what he was told. The beaver tied the other end to a nearby tree and ran back to the bear.

'Pull with all your might, Bear,' she said. The bear used all of his great strength, but he was still stuck. He placed his paws higher on the vine and tried again. This time, inch by inch, he began to come out of the quicksand slowly. Eventually he managed to pull himself clear.

When he recovered he thanked the beaver for such quick thinking. Turning to the monkey and owl he was cross and said, 'Why didn't you help me, like the beaver?'

Follow-up questions

◆ If someone needs help it is best to help them and not just talk about it. Can you think of a time when you have helped someone?
◆ How did it make you feel?
◆ Which animal did the right thing and why?

Brilliant Stories for Assemblies
© Paul Urry

How the kingfisher got its beautiful feathers

(Africa)

Props suggested
A picture of an English kingfisher, possibly other kingfishers from around the world.

On the banks of a muddy river lived a small brown fisher bird. None of the other animals even noticed it. It used to dive into the water to get small fish and sit on a branch from where it would watch the clever snake, the proud tiger and the acrobatic monkeys.

One day, as the fisher bird was watching the forest, he heard a noise in the distance. Snake said to Tiger, 'The king is coming. We must go and greet him. He wears the most beautiful clothes.'

'His gown is decorated with the finest and most colourful feathers. He has jewellery of every description,' the monkeys added excitedly.

As the royal procession came near the river the animals jumped out to greet the great king. The king's horse was scared when he saw the animals and reared up in fright. The king was a good horseman and stayed seated but his ring was knocked from his finger. As the animals and servants looked in horror, the ring flew in the air and landed in the middle of the river.

The king was furious. 'Who dares to scare my horse? Where has my ring gone? Go and get it!' he demanded.

The animals all looked at each other, unsure what to do.

'I will find your ring,' roared Tiger, and he swam out into the river. 'The river is too deep. I cannot feel the ring,' he said swimming back.

'We will climb the trees and look from high up,' the monkeys said confidently. From the branches they looked down into the river, but it was too muddy.

Snake slithered into the river and swam under the water. Try as he might he could not find the ring. The king raged with anger at the animals.

'I can help,' said a small voice. The fisher bird flew onto the head of the king's horse. 'I can get your ring,' he said.

'I will grant you any wish if you can,' said the king.

With that the fisher bird flew high into the air and dived into the water. Within seconds he emerged from the water with the ring in his beak.

The king was overjoyed. 'Tell me what you want, little bird.'

'All I ask is for some of your brightly coloured feathers so that I will not be just a dull brown bird ever again.'

'Is that all?' the king said. 'You have done me a great favour. You shall have some of my beautiful feathers, but from this day on you shall not be known as just a fisher bird but the king's fisher.'

The kingfisher gave a big smile and flew off with his new feathers.

Follow-up question
◆ Everyone has a gift. Think of a skill that you have. How could you use it to help other people?

Brilliant Stories for Assemblies
© Paul Urry

This page may be photocopied by the purchasing institution only.

9

Grandpa and the wave
(Japan)

Props suggested
World map to show where Japan is.

A long time ago in a village in Japan there lived an old man. He lived a quiet life. Some days he would tell the children stories from long ago; on others he would sit by himself and watch nature, the villagers and the world.

On one particular hot day the old man was sitting under a tree in a cool breeze. He was watching the villagers in the rice fields starting to gather the crop when suddenly the ground shook. It shook for what seemed an age, and then stopped – an earthquake. Nobody in the village worried, they were used to earthquakes, and this one was a small one. So they carried on with their work in the village.

The old man, however, was worried. He stood up and looked out to sea. He stared at the horizon in the distance, then his normally calm expression changed. There was panic on his face. He picked up his walking stick and walked down to the fields.

'Come with me to the top of the mountain, we are all in great danger!' he tried to shout, but his voice was too weak and the people were working too hard. He tried again to shout, but no one was listening. In desperation he took a plant, lit it and threw it into the rice crop. The plants caught fire quickly.

Panicking, the people ran up the mountain for safety. They knew that when the crops caught fire on a hot day there was nothing that they could do.

'Now we will have no food for the winter,' they complained.

Eventually all the villagers were at the top of the mountain looking down at their village and their rice fields on fire.

'Who started this?' demanded the village leader.

From the back of the crowd the old man came forward. 'I did,' he said. 'I had to. Nobody could hear me.'

'Why?' they all asked.

'Because you ignored the earthquake,' the old man explained.

'It was only a small one,' the leader said. 'It did no harm.'

'It was not a land earthquake,' he continued, 'but a sea one. I watched the water and saw what was going to happen and had to get you up here.'

'Look!' a boy shouted, pointing out to sea. As they were listening to the old man the sea had begun to change shape. Slowly the waves died down and, in the distance, a giant wave appeared, getting closer to the beach.

'A tidal wave,' the old man explained. The villagers could only watch as the giant wave came crashing down on the village, destroying homes and putting out the fire.

(continued on next page)

Brilliant Stories for Assemblies
© Paul Urry

'We would all have died if it hadn't been for you, old man,' the leader said, and with that they all travelled down the mountain cheering and celebrating.

Follow-up questions

◆ Was the old man right to set fire to the food?

◆ Do you think that he was clever?

Peter and the wolf
(Russia)

Note: This story can be acted out as a class assembly using just the music of Prokofiev, or having the children in masks or labels, thus providing an excellent introduction to classical music. Below is a suggested narrative for each of the seventeen sections of the story. Use the narrative first followed by the music so that the children can imagine what is going on.

This is the story of a boy called Peter who lived with his grandfather long ago in Russia. Each of the main characters in the story is associated with a particular instrument:

Note: the instruments used as as follows:
- bird   *flute*
- duck   *oboe*
- cat   *clarinet*
- grandfather   *bassoon*
- wolf   *horn*
- Peter   *strings*
- rifles   *drums*

1. One morning Peter went through the gate of his garden into a field.
2. On a tree sat a bird who spoke happily to Peter.
3. A duck came by and waddled into a pond.
4. The bird took off, landed near the duck and asked why it couldn't fly. The duck said, 'Why can't you swim?'
5. Peter's grandfather came running out of the house. 'Don't go out into the field, Peter,' he said crossly. 'A wolf may come out.' But Peter just shrugged his shoulders and followed him back to the garden.
6. As soon as he was back in the garden a wolf did come out of the wood.
7. The cat quickly climbed the tree.
8. The duck panicked, jumped out of the pond and tried to run away.
9. But the wolf was too fast for the duck. He caught the duck and quickly ate it whole.
10. The cat and the bird sat in the tree watching the wolf, walking around the tree, waiting to eat them.
11. Peter watched from the safety of his gate. He ran into the house and got a piece of rope and climbed the stone wall. He could reach one of the branches of the tree from the wall. He grabbed the branch and climbed onto the tree.
12. Peter said to the bird, 'Carefully fly around the wolf's head.' The wolf tried to catch the bird, but couldn't.
13. Meanwhile Peter made a lasso, trapped the wolf by the tail and pulled with all his strength. The wolf tried to escape. As the wolf struggled, Peter tied the other end of the rope to the tree.
14. From the woods, some hunters who had been following the wolf appeared firing their guns.
15. 'Don't shoot!' shouted Peter. 'I have captured him. Let's take him to the zoo.'
16. Everyone lined up, with Peter at the front … then the hunters, the wolf, the grandfather and finally the cat and the bird.
17. And, if you are quiet, you can hear the sound of the duck quacking inside the wolf, because he had swallowed her … alive!

Follow-up questions
- Why do you think Peter was so brave?
- Did the different instruments remind you of the characters?

Brilliant Stories for Assemblies
© Paul Urry

Robert the Bruce

(Scotland)

Props suggested

Picture of the statue of Robert the Bruce.
A plastic spider hanging from a thread.

Nearly seven hundred years ago lived a brave king of Scotland. His name was Robert the Bruce. At that time, Scotland and England fought each other in battles. The English had beaten Robert in the last five battles.

In the sixth one, the English made the Scots run away in different directions. Robert himself had had to escape or he would have been killed. He found safety in some woods. There he found a cave where he could keep warm and dry.

Whilst he was there he thought about the battles and how he had finally been beaten. Sitting down and leaning against the wall of the cave, he noticed a small spider hanging from the roof. In the darkness he watched as it hung from its fine thread and tried to swing across to the other side of the cave to start its web.

Robert sat there and saw that, on the first swing, the spider nearly made it. On its second attempt it managed to get one leg onto the wall, but slipped off. A third time it tried and again it did not make it. Robert kept watching, fascinated by the perseverance of this small creature. It tried a fourth, fifth and sixth time and still it did not make it.

'Why don't you give up, my small friend? You and I are the same. We cannot win. Know when to stop. I have.'

But the spider continued and, as Robert watched him, he finally managed to get to the far side of the cave wall.

Robert sat in amazement. *If something as small as a spider did not give up, then why should I?* And with that he got up and confidently walked from the cave. He appealed to all the leaders of the Scottish clans and told them that they would try once more to defeat the English.

He gathered all his men at a place called Bannockburn, just outside the city of Stirling. There he attacked and won a great victory, forcing the English out of Scotland. Robert became a great and famous leader. But he knew that he had been ready to give up and stop and, if it had not been for one of the smallest and weakest creatures, the spider, he would have done so.

Today in Bannockburn, there is a fantastic statue of Robert riding his horse with all his chain mail on so that people will never forget him.

Follow-up questions

◆ Should Robert have given up after trying six times?
◆ Can you think of something you want to give up doing but know that you really should persevere with?

Brilliant Stories for Assemblies
© Paul Urry

This page may be photocopied by the purchasing institution only.

13

The caliph, the beggar and the judge
(Iraq)

A long time ago, a caliph, or king, decided to travel to see his kingdom. He was a wise and clever caliph and wanted to disguise himself so that nobody would see who he was.

As he travelled he saw a beggar. He felt for the man and gave him some money and said to him that he could ride on his horse to the next village. The beggar climbed on and they travelled together.

'We are here now,' said the caliph, 'You can get off first.'

To his surprise the beggar said. 'No, it is my horse now, you get off!'

The caliph was furious. 'How dare you! After I have helped you. No-one will believe it is your horse.'

'Why not?' the beggar said slyly. 'We are both strangers in this town.'

The caliph knew he was right, but he was determined not to give in. 'I will go to the judge,' he said, 'and we will let him decide.'

Both men went to the courtroom and told the judge their story.

'I helped this man,' said the caliph, 'and this is how he repays me.'

'What?' complained the beggar. 'I have always had this horse. I need it because I cannot walk easily.'

The judge thought for a while. 'Leave the horse with me and I will decide tomorrow.'

The next day the caliph and the beggar went into the courtroom. The judge sat in his chair and, looking at the caliph, said, 'Take your horse, and continue your journey.'

To the beggar he said, 'How dare you try to steal from someone who tried to help you. You are a greedy person, who must learn to work for yourself and help others just as this man has helped you. Guards! Take him to the prison until he learns his lesson.'

The caliph was extremely impressed with the judge. 'How did you know that the horse was mine?' he asked.

The judge laughed. 'It was easy. When I had the guards take your horse away, I left it in a stable outside. When the beggar walked past the stable, the horse did nothing. But when you walked past, he lifted his head and started neighing. Only the owner of this horse would make him do this.'

'You are indeed a wise and fair man,' the caliph said, 'but there is one thing you don't know.'

'What?' the judge asked, puzzled.

The caliph removed his disguise. The judge recognized him and fell to his knees. 'Oh great ruler. I am sorry if I have upset you.'

'Upset me?' he laughed, as he helped the judge to his feet. 'You will come back with me to my palace and become my chief judge.'

Follow-up question
◆ Why did the beggar try to steal the horse?

Brilliant Stories for Assemblies
© Paul Urry

George Washington and the cherry tree
(USA)

Props suggested

Picture of George Washington. His clothes and the fact it is a painting, not a photograph, will help to show that the story is over 200 years old.

George Washington was the first president of the United States of America. This is a famous story, but some people think it was made up to show what a fair man he was. It is still told in schools to show how good he was.

George Washington grew up on a farm. On the farm was a special cherry tree that his father liked. George liked to help around the farm so, on one of his birthdays, he got an axe. George loved the axe and helped cut branches and trees that weren't needed.

George went around the farm chopping trees and large branches. One day he walked up to the cherry tree, lifted the axe up high and hit the tree trunk. He took his axe out again and kept chopping until eventually the tree started to fall. As he watched, George realized that he had cut down his father's favourite cherry tree.

The next day his father noticed that his tree had been cut down. He saw that there were axe marks on the tree trunk. He was angry and called for George.

As George came over his father asked him, 'Do you know who cut down my cherry tree?'

George thought about what to say. He could see how angry his father was. What should he do – tell a lie and not get punished or tell the truth because it is the right thing to do?

(The story can be stopped here for a discussion about what he should do or what the children would do if they were in his place. Then continue with the story.)

After thinking, George said, 'Father, I cannot tell a lie. I chopped down the tree.'

His father's anger was replaced with pride that, instead of telling a lie, George had decided to tell the truth.

Today in America, on the third Thursday of February, Americans celebrate this story by eating lots of cherry pies!

Follow-up questions
◆ Why did George tell the truth?
◆ Why do Americans celebrate his life?

Brilliant Stories for Assemblies
© Paul Urry

This page may be photocopied by the purchasing institution only.

15

The king of the birds
(Southern Africa)

Before people lived on earth all the birds gathered in one place.

'We must choose a king,' said the eagle.

All the other birds looked at each other and agreed.

The eagle stood proudly in front of them. 'I am the strongest flying bird. I have great claws and a sharp beak. It should be me!' he declared.

The other birds looked at each other. The eagle certainly was a fearsome creature. But not everyone was happy.

'Oh no,' said the owl, 'I have the largest eyes of any bird. I can see all that happens. It should be me.'

'I have the largest wings of all the birds,' said the buzzard confidently. 'It should be me.'

There was a great deal of arguing amongst all the birds. When it eventually died down a small voice was heard.

'I may not be fierce like the eagle, or have big eyes like the owl or even be as tall as the ostrich, but why shouldn't I be king of the birds,' said a small brown warbler.

The birds started laughing at the small bird. How could he be king? He was so small and useless.

As the crowd got quieter the eagle said, 'We are not going to agree, so we need a competition. The bird that can fly the highest shall be the king of the birds!' Everyone thought that was fair and it was agreed. All the birds gathered together. The warbler knew that he could not fly as high as the other great birds so he decided to hide in the feathers of the great eagle.

With a flourish all the birds took off together. As they climbed higher and higher in the sky, the exhausted smaller birds had to give up and fly back to earth. As they watched from the ground, they could see other birds giving up.

Eventually only three were left – the eagle, the owl and the buzzard. The owl was now getting more and more tired and had to stop. The buzzard's wings ached and he too gave up.

'You win, Eagle,' he said.

The eagle was also exhausted but, just as he was going to give up, the warbler flew from his feathers and announced, 'I am the winner!'

Try as he might the eagle could not fly any further.

As the warbler flew down to earth the other birds, rather than being happy for him, were furious.

(continued on next page)

'You have cheated!' they shouted, and chased him into the woods, where he still lives today.

As for the rest of the birds, they are still arguing about who should be king!

Follow-up questions

◆ Was the warbler right to cheat?
◆ Did he like the eagle?
◆ Who do you think should have been chosen as king?

The kind man
(India)

A long time ago a hard-working and thoughtful man lived in India. He made sure that he always saved some of the money he earned working in the fields, after he had spent some on food and clothes. Whenever he got paid, he took out the spare coins and put them in a jar underneath his bed.

After several years the man wondered how much money he had collected. To his surprise he saw that, because he had been careful not to spend all his money, he was rich.

'What should I do with all this money?' he thought. 'I don't need it. I know – I should give it to someone who likes nice things.' And with that he bought a beautiful piece of jewellery.

Talking to a traveller one day he said, 'Who is the most beautiful woman in the world?'

'That is simple,' said the traveller. 'I see many people and everyone talks about a princess who lives at the palace.'

'Good,' said the man. 'Would you be kind enough to give her this?' And he gave the traveller the piece of jewellery.

The princess was overjoyed when she saw such beautiful jewellery. 'I must give him something in return,' she said. 'Fetch me two handsome horses.' She asked the traveller to give the horses to the kind man.

'Oh no!' said the kind man. 'I don't want anything. I just want to give my money away. I do not need it. I am happy here. Please, traveller, take the horses to the queen.' And the traveller did.

When the queen saw the horses she said, 'These are fine horses indeed. The man must be trying to please me. Well he has. Take these pots of silver to him.'

'Not again!' cried the kind man. 'Didn't you tell the queen I don't want anything? I just want to be left alone. Dear traveller, please keep one jar of silver for yourself and take the rest to the king. Tell him to use the silver to help people.' Again the traveller did as he was asked.

'I did not know we had such rich people in my kingdom,' the king announced, smiling. 'Bring this man to me so that I can say thank you to his face and he can live with us at the palace.'

The traveller returned again and told the man to go to the palace.

When the man arrived the king, queen and princess were overjoyed to meet him. They said he could have anything he wanted. The man thought for a while, he saw the magnificent palace and the great riches there. But eventually he asked to return to the fields where he could work in peace.

Surprised, the king granted his wish. The man was happy now and continued his quiet life working in the fields .

Follow-up questions
◆ Why was the man happy to stay working?
◆ Do you think he was sensible?

This page may be photocopied by the purchasing institution only.

18

Brilliant Stories for Assemblies
© Paul Urry

Greyfriars Bobby
(Scotland)

About a hundred and fifty years ago a policeman lived in Edinburgh, in Scotland. His name was John Gray. Old Jock, as he was known, lived in the area of Edinburgh called Greyfriars.

One day he decided that he needed a watchdog, to walk the streets with him and keep him company. Old Jock and his new dog, Bobby, became very close. Whenever the policeman left his house, Bobby would follow.

When Bobby was two years old, his life changed. Old Jock became very ill and, late one night, he died. Bobby couldn't understand what had happened. He saw lots of people come into the house and, eventually, he saw his master being taken away.

He followed the people to the church, chasing after them and barking. He heard lots of people singing and, when they came out of the church, he saw the coffin go into the ground.

Bobby stayed by the grave all night. The warden chased him away and locked the gate, but Bobby jumped over the wall and lay by Old Jock's grave. Every night he would be chased away and every night he would return to the grave, curl up and go to sleep. Some days it rained heavily and was windy. Still Bobby remained, shivering.

People in the area used to come and see him sitting near Old Jock's grave. Some brought him food, in particular the owner of a small restaurant. In Edinburgh at one o'clock every day a cannon is fired from the castle. When Bobby heard this he used to leave the graveyard and run to the restaurant, where there would be some food for him. After eating, he would return to the graveside. Even in winter, when the snow covered the ground, Bobby would stay by Old Jock. Some people tried to keep him indoors when it was really cold, but Bobby would bark and bark until they let him out so that he could return to the grave.

This continued for nine years. Local children would go up to him and stroke him. However, it was found out that Bobby did not have a licence. The person who owned the restaurant was arrested, but people complained and the man was released. When the judge heard about the case he went to see Bobby. He was so amazed at this little dog that he paid for the licence himself and said that Bobby could go wherever in the city he wanted.

After fourteen years of staying by the graveside, Bobby died. A long article appeared in the newspaper about him. He was buried next to Old Jock and a statue was erected near the graveyard.

Today if you go to Edinburgh, on Candlemakers Row near Greyfriars Churchyard, there is a statue of a dog, Greyfriars Bobby.

Follow-up questions
◆ Why did Bobby stay by the graveside?
◆ Why do you think people liked Bobby?

Brilliant Stories for Assemblies
© Paul Urry

This page may be photocopied by the purchasing institution only.

19

Johnny Appleseed
(USA)

Props suggested
An apple, which can be cut open to reveal the seeds. Map of the USA. Picture of Johnny.

Note: This story is told throughout the USA. It is about leading a simple life, supporting the environment and helping others.

On 26th September 1774 a boy named John Chapman was born in America. When he grew up he used to take the seeds from the middle of apples and then plant them. When they grew into small saplings he sold them, keeping some of the trees himself to continue growing and producing more apples.

About two hundred years ago when he lived, America was a very different place from what it is today. Most people lived in only a small part of the east coast. As more people came to America, they started to spread out towards the Great Lakes and further inland towards the huge Mississippi river.

Johnny grew up in an area now called New York, but he loved to travel. He used to find a good piece of ground and plant hundreds, sometimes thousands, of apple seeds. All his trees grew in neat straight lines and he always built a fence around them to protect them from wild animals.

It was a dangerous time to live; people were often killed or had things stolen from them, but Johnny never carried a gun and people came from miles around to buy some of his apple trees. Everyone knew this kind and friendly man. He soon became known as Johnny Appleseed.

Johnny lived a very simple life. He had no home of his own as he kept moving from place to place. His clothes were often torn because he worked outside in the fields all the time and he did not make a lot of money to keep himself. All he carried around with him were a pot for cooking and a kettle. In lots of pictures he is seen with the pot on his head! Sometimes he would even give trees away to people who had no money. Lots of people used to invite him into their houses to give him something to eat and a warm bed to sleep.

Although he made lots of new friends, he always wanted to move on and explore. As the trees grew, Johnny would collect some of the seeds, carefully put them in a bag and then move on to a different part of America and start all over again, planting the seeds and building fences.

The story of Johnny and his apple trees travelled throughout America before there were televisions or newspapers. People think that he planted MILLIONS of trees. Some of these apple orchards can still be found today in parts of America. Americans love eating apples – one of their favourite types of food is still apple pie!

Follow-up questions
◆ Do you think Johnny should have tried to make more money from his trees?
◆ Would you have given apples away, even though you had worked so hard to grow them?

Brilliant Stories for Assemblies
© Paul Urry

How the years were named
(China)

Props suggested
Pictures or masks of each animal
(this story can be acted out effectively).
Calendars showing the Christian and
Chinese years.

'I think the year should be named after me,' declared the ox. 'After all, I help people plough their fields.'

'What!' roared the tiger. 'I am the greatest of all animals. People look at my strength and respect me.'

'You may be strong, Tiger,' pointed out the cockerel, 'but without me, people wouldn't get up in the morning.'

The other animals were not happy with this. 'We all deserve the year to be named after us.'

Rat, Snake, Horse, Monkey, Sheep, Rabbit, Dog, Dragon and even Pig all had good arguments too for having the year named after them. As they shouted, the noise got louder and louder. Eventually the gods were disturbed and asked the animals what was the matter. Ox explained that each of the twelve animals there wanted the year to be named after them.

The gods thought for a while. 'Do you see that river in the distance?' they asked. 'Well, if you all line up on this bank and race across it, the winner shall have the year named after them.'

All the animals liked this idea, except Rat. Rat knew that the much bigger animals were faster and stronger than he was. So he had to think of a plan.

All the animals lined up on one side of the river. Rat carefully stood next to Ox.

'Go!' shouted the gods.

All of the animals jumped into the river and started to swim. As Ox jumped, Rat grabbed hold of his tail and carefully pulled himself up onto Ox's back. Ox was so busy concentrating on swimming that he did not feel the small rat on him.

The animals swam with all their might, determined to be the first one on the other side of the river, but Ox was in the lead. Nearer and nearer they got to the other side. Ox was about to get out of the water first when Rat jumped onto his head and onto the other side.

'I won!' he shouted.

Ox was furious that Rat had cheated. All the other animals and gods laughed at the clever rat.

'We didn't say you had to swim,' they said. 'The year shall be named after Rat, but after that each year will be named after each animal as they finished in the race. When all twelve animals have had their turn it will be Rat's again.'

All the animals agreed to this. In third place, after Rat and Ox, came Tiger. Fourth was Rabbit, fifth Dragon, sixth Snake, seventh Horse, eighth Sheep, ninth Monkey, tenth Cockerel, eleventh was Dog and last was the laziest, Pig.

Follow-up questions
◆ Was Rat right to stay on Ox's back?
◆ Do you know the Chinese year in which you were born?

Brilliant Stories for Assemblies
© Paul Urry

This page may be photocopied by the purchasing institution only.

21

Anansi and Tiger
(Jamaica)

There are many stories about Anansi the spider. Sometimes he is clever or brave. Other times he makes mistakes and looks silly. In this story we find out why all stories are named after him.

One warm night, when all the animals were gathered round, they listened to the stories of Tiger, the strongest and fiercest animal. At the end of the stories Anansi asked, 'Could the stories be named after me, not you, Tiger?'

The other animals fell around laughing. 'You!' they cried. 'You are the weakest animal. What can you do?'

But to their surprise Tiger said 'Of course.' The animals stopped laughing, stunned, but Tiger continued, 'You need to do two things though. Firstly bring me a hive of bees and honey and secondly bring me the great Snake alive.'

The animals carried on laughing. 'One bee sting would kill the spider and, anyway, how could one so small trap the powerful Snake?'

Anansi did not laugh, though. Instead he simply said, 'I will.'

The next day, Anansi took a jar to a hive.

'Oh dear! Oh dear!' he kept on saying.

'What's up, Anansi?' asked the queen bee.

'Tiger bet me that I couldn't find out how many bees I could get in this jar,' Anansi lied.

'I will help,' said the queen bee. 'I will tell the bees to fly into the jar and you can count.'

And so they started to fly into the jar. When the jar was almost full, Anansi got a lid and put it on the jar. Taking it to Tiger he said, 'Here is your hive of bees.'

Tiger was furious: 'You still need to bring mighty Snake to me … alive!'

'I know.' said Anansi, and crawled away.

The next day, Anansi walked down to the river with a knife to where Snake lived.

'What are you doing?' asked Snake.

'I cannot tell you,' Anansi said.

'If you don't tell me, I will eat you,' Snake hissed.

'OK then,' Anansi said. 'Tiger said you were shorter than the great bamboo plant.'

'Rubbish!' Snake shouted. 'I am far longer.'

'I know,' Anansi lied, 'but I need to find out.'

'Use your knife and cut down the tallest bamboo,' demanded Snake.

Anansi did this and said, 'I need to tie your head to one end to stop you cheating.' Snake let him. 'Snake, you are shorter. Stretch.' Snake made himself as long as he could. Anansi continued to tie him to the bamboo so tightly that he could not escape.

The other animals came to see what all the noise was.

(continued on next page)

Brilliant Stories for Assemblies
© Paul Urry

'Nearly there,' shouted Anansi.

Finally, Tiger came to see what the noise was, just as Anansi was tying Snake's tail to the bamboo. 'One mighty snake … alive!'

The other animals cheered as Tiger walked away, knowing that he had been beaten.

Follow-up question
◆ Was Anansi right to lie?

The seven horses
(Norway)

Once there was a poor couple who lived in a hut in a wood with their two sons. One day the elder son said he wanted to go into the city and earn some money. As he walked through the gates, he saw the king.

'Will you work for me and look after my seven horses?' asked the king. 'If you can I will let you marry my daughter.'

The elder son could not believe his luck. What a great prize for such a simple task!

Early the next morning he got up and the king let the horses out. The son ran all around making sure he stayed with them. Eventually, though, he became tired.

'Would you like some water and bread?' an old lady called out to him.

'Yes please,' said the elder son, 'but I need to look after these horses.'

'Don't worry, they will be back,' she said.

As evening came, the seven horses did come back and the son led them into the stables.

'Well done,' said the king. 'If you have really stayed with them all day you can tell me what they ate.'

'Grass and water, of course.'

The king knew he was lying and had his guards chase him out of the city and back to the woods. The son told his family what had happened.

That night the younger son secretly packed some bread and water and set off for the city. Next morning he also met the king, who asked him to look after his horses. The boy agreed and also chased them all over the fields. He too got tired. As before, the old lady called out to him.

'No! I must complete my job. I have my own food and water,' and with that he continued to chase the horses.

One horse stopped and said, 'Get on my back.'

The boy did and he and the horses galloped to a nearby town. As they approached a bakery all the horses changed into princes. They bought some bread and wine and told the son a secret. As they left the bakery they changed back into horses and galloped back to the stables.

'Well done,' said the king. 'If you have stayed with them all day you can tell me what they ate.'

The son told the king the story.

'Well done!' he said, 'You are a clever young man and may marry my daughter.'

The wedding was quickly arranged and there was a great celebration. During the feast, though, the son left the room and went down to the stables. There he drew his sword and, one by one, cut the heads off each horse, just as they had asked him to do at the bakery. As he cut the final head off, all the horses changed into princes.

'You have broken the spell,' they cheered. 'Thank you.'

The son returned to the hall and continued the feast, quietly smiling to himself.

Follow-up questions
◆ Why didn't the boy tell anyone what he did? Do you think he was clever?

Brilliant Stories for Assemblies
© Paul Urry

Babushka
(Russia)

In a house deep in a wood lived an old lady called Babushka. She lived all alone and did not see many people. During the winter in Russia it gets very cold and the snow is so deep that you cannot walk through it. This did not bother Babushka. She spent her time cleaning, cooking and doing jobs around the house. She was happy and never felt lonely.

One particularly cold night in winter, Babushka was surprised to hear voices outside in the wood. She carefully opened the door, a little scared that they might be robbers, but to her surprise, she saw three men. They wore extremely expensive clothes and looked cold and hungry.

'Please come in, gentlemen,' she said politely. She made up a nice roaring fire to keep them warm and went off to the kitchen to make some vegetable soup.

'You are very kind,' one man said. 'How much do we owe you for all this?'

'Don't be silly. I am happy to help. Anyway, where are you going on such a terrible night like this?' she asked.

'We are searching for a baby prince. We were following a star, but we could not see it tonight because of the snowstorm.'

'Why don't you stay on the roads, then, rather than walk through dark woods?'

'We go only where the star leads us,' they said. 'We have to follow the star because we have expensive gifts for him. He is special.'

'Could I see him too?' she wondered.

'Of course! You have been very kind to us. Why don't you join us?'

'No, I'm afraid I'm too old for such a journey. I will slow you down.'

As the men looked out of the window, they saw that the snow was clearing. Warm and well fed, they thanked Babushka and set off again, following the star.

When they had left, Babushka felt lonely and lost for the first time. She decided that she should go with the visitors. Quickly, she ran around her house and collected some food, clothes and toys for the baby prince.

The next day she set off and tried to catch up with her visitors but, every time she asked, people said they had left that town and moved on.

Babushka never caught up with the travellers and never saw the royal prince. In Russia people believe that she stills travels all over Russia giving all the babies she meets presents.

Follow-up questions
- Who were the visitors and the prince?
- Do you think that Babushka was a happy or sad character?

Brilliant Stories for Assemblies
© Paul Urry

This page may be photocopied by the purchasing institution only.

25

The rich man and the beggar
(Christianity)

Note: This parable is taken from Luke 16:19–31.

Jesus told many parables. These are stories that help us understand something difficult. In many examples he tries to describe God's love for people, what heaven is like, or how we should behave towards each other. This example is about the last type – how Jesus wants us to live our lives.

Jesus said …

There was once a rich man who had a very comfortable life. He had good clothes and good food. Every day was a luxury. He did not have to worry about anything. At the gate of his house, however, lay a beggar. His name was Lazarus. He did not have enough money to buy food and relied on food he could find or that was thrown out. He wore old, dirty clothes and had sores all over his body. As he lay there near the gates, dogs would come up to him and lick his sores and spread infections. Lazarus had a miserable life.

The rich man knew about Lazarus as he passed him when he went in and out of his gates, but he did nothing, just ignored him.

Years later the beggar died and went to heaven. There he sat by Abraham. The rich man soon died as well, but he went to hell. Looking up he saw the beggar by the side of Abraham.

'Father Abraham, please ask the beggar to send down water. I'm in agony in this fire.'

Abraham replied, 'Why should he help you? When you were alive you had everything and he had nothing, but you did not help him then. Anyway, it is impossible to pass between heaven and hell.'

Knowing the mistakes he had made the rich man pleaded again.

'Father Abraham, please send Lazarus to my father and five brothers. Let him tell them to do the right thing and change how they live and treat others. I know it is too late for me, but please don't make it too late for them. They will listen to a spirit.'

But Abraham replied, 'They do not need Lazarus. They have the words of the prophets, just like you had. If they choose to ignore them, like you did, then that is their choice. If they do not know God now, a spirit will not change their mind.'

Follow-up questions
◆ Why was the rich man punished?
◆ Do you think it was fair he was punished?
◆ What do you think he could have done differently?

Brilliant Stories for Assemblies
© Paul Urry

Miracle: Ten healed of leprosy
(Christianity)

Note: Taken from Luke 17:11–19

In the Gospels there are thirty-five examples of Jesus healing people. Many people believed that Jesus was God when they saw these miracles. Jesus did not announce that he could do these things. Nor did he boast and tell others. He simply did them. In this example Jesus heals ten people in one go.

Whilst on his way to Jerusalem, Jesus passed through a village. In the village he came across ten men who had a skin disease, called leprosy. The men did not want to walk up to Jesus because they were not allowed to go up to anyone in case they passed on their disease. They called out instead.

'Jesus, master, have pity on us!'

Jesus saw the men and saw their disease. 'Go show yourselves to your priests,' he said. Now at that time only a priest, not a doctor, would say if you were cured or not.

As they travelled to see the priest, they noticed that their skin was healing – just by the word of Jesus.

'We have come to show you we are healed,' they said to the priest.

The priest was careful at first as he knew these people, and knew that they had been ill for a long time. But when he looked closer, he noticed that they were, in fact, healed. He checked all of them one after the other and saw that they were fine.

The men all celebrated and ran into the village. One, however, stopped and went back where he had come from to find Jesus.

'Praise be to God!' shouted the man. 'I have been cured by God.' When he saw Jesus he immediately threw himself at the feet of Jesus because he was allowed to go up to him now.

'Thank you, Lord,' he said. 'I can carry on with my life now thanks to you.'

Jesus asked, 'Didn't I cure all ten? Where are the other nine? Why haven't they returned to praise God as you have done?'

Jesus picked the man up and said, 'Rise and go, your faith has made you a well man.'

And with that the man ran off, continuing to praise God.

Follow-up questions
- Why didn't the other men return to see Jesus?
- How do you think Jesus felt about this?
- Did he want the people to say thank you?

Brilliant Stories for Assemblies
© Paul Urry

This page may be photocopied by the purchasing institution only.

27

Palm Sunday
(Christianity)

Props suggested
Palm leaves made from paper, to show the size. Palm cross. Map to show where Galilee, Bethlehem and Jerusalem are.

Note: Taken from Matthew 21; 1–11, Mark 11: 1–10, Luke 19: 29–40 and John 12: 12–19.

Jesus had, for the previous three years, been travelling, teaching people about God, performing miracles and telling people about heaven. He had become famous as the man from Galilee in the north. Before the time of television, photographs and newspapers, people told information to others and they then passed it on.

Now, news had spread that Jesus was close to Jerusalem, the most important city in the area, where the Roman and religious leaders lived. If he walked into Jerusalem he would be taking a great risk. Jesus knew this and knew that he was going to be arrested and killed. However, the people around him did not know this. This was only a week before he would rise from the dead.

He wanted to enter Jerusalem. Should he enter as a king on a fantastic horse? No, he was not a king and did not want to be seen like one. Instead, Jesus said to two of his disciples, 'Go to the village ahead of you and you will see a donkey. Untie the donkey. If anyone asks you why you are taking it say that the Lord needs it.'

The disciples did what they were asked and found the donkey. The owner did ask what they were doing but let them have it when they explained who it was for.

Jesus sat on the donkey and entered the city through one of its gates. When people saw who it was there was great excitement. They shouted from their houses, 'Hosanna to the son of David!' (David was one of the great kings of Israel.)

They pulled huge branches from the palm trees and waved them in the air. People came from all over the city to see what was happening.

'This is Jesus,' they cheered, 'the prophet from Nazareth in Galilee.'

Follow-up questions
◆ Why did the crowd behave like this?
◆ Only five days later, Jesus was crucified. Do you know why?

Brilliant Stories for Assemblies
© Paul Urry

St. George
(Christianity)

Props suggested
Flag of St. George. Map showing the countries involved.

Just over two hundred years after Jesus lived, a baby boy was born in Turkey. His name was George. He came from a rich family and his father was a great ruler. He trained to be a soldier in the Roman army. George became a brave and respected leader. However, while he was still young he saw a vision of Jesus, who told him to tell others about Christianity. This changed George's life for ever. He gave up everything he owned and left the army. He began to travel around the Roman Empire telling everyone of the greatness of God and Jesus.

The most famous story about him starts in an area of North Africa, today called Libya. He heard about a dragon that was terrorising a city. Every day the city had to feed the dragon two sheep. However, when the sheep were all gone, they had to sacrifice young men and women of the area for the dragon to eat.

While he was travelling, George heard a young lady crying. She was tied to a post to stop her running away. He asked her what was wrong and she told him that she was waiting to be eaten by the dragon. He drew his sword from his belt and told the people of the city that Jesus would give him the strength to kill the dragon. He went to the dragon's cave and fought bravely against the fire-breathing monster. Eventually, with the dragon and George both getting tired from the fight, he dived underneath the dragon's head and drove his sword deep into its heart. With a loud cry, the dragon fell to the ground, dead.

The people of the city were so impressed with George that they listened to his stories of Jesus and became Christians.

On returning to his home he heard about a king who wanted all the local leaders to worship pictures. George decided to go there and tell them about Jesus. When George arrived he impressed all the people but the local leader had him thrown into prison. They tortured him but he kept saying that Jesus would give him strength. He converted many people in prison to Christianity. They tried to poison him, but that did not kill him. Eventually, the king decided to have George's head cut off.

When people found out what had happened, they were not sad. Instead they celebrated the greatness of George. Many became Christians when they heard of his bravery.

A thousand years later an English king, Richard I, had a vision of George before a great battle. He told his army to follow the example of George and fight for Jesus. He held George's flag up – a red cross on a white background – and won a great victory.

Because of his faith in God and his bravery, it was decided to have a day of celebration to mark his life on 23rd April

(continued on next page)

Brilliant Stories for Assemblies
© Paul Urry

This page may be photocopied by the purchasing institution only.

29

Follow-up questions

St. George's faith changed people's lives and helped him help others in need.

- ◆ How can this story help us think about others?
- ◆ Why is he patron saint of England?

Brilliant Stories for Assemblies
© Paul Urry

St. David
(Christianity)

Props suggested
- Map of South Wales, showing St. David's.
- A picture of the small cathedral there.

St. David was born over one and a half thousand years ago in Wales. His father was a prince. He was taught by a blind monk about Christianity. This changed David's life. There are many stories about David's ability to perform miracles. When he was young he made the sign of the cross with his hands at a monk and instantly cured him of his blindness. The monk realized that David was a great person and sent him all over Wales to tell people about Jesus. At different places all around Wales he had monasteries built, where people could pray and read the Bible. Some people, monks, chose to stay there all their lives. David was a very strict leader. He made all the monks at his monasteries drink only water and talk to each other only when it was important. He made them get up early in the morning to pray and sing to God. When people found out that David was in their area they would rush out to hear him speak about Jesus.

In one miracle told about David, the crowd was so big that not everyone could see him. David placed a handkerchief on the ground and suddenly it grew beneath him, until he was standing on a small hill.

David lived to be a very old man. He died on 1st March 589. Hundreds of years later, when people had forgotten about him, a book was written telling everyone about his great achievements.

It was decided that David should be made the patron (special) saint of Wales and he should be celebrated on the day he died.

Today people travel to St. David's Cathedral in a part of Wales called Pembrokeshire, where St. David is buried.

Follow-up questions
- Could you have been a monk with David?
- Would it have been too strict?
- Why do you think people listened to David and converted to Christianity?

Brilliant Stories for Assemblies
© Paul Urry

This page may be photocopied by the purchasing institution only.

31

St. Andrew
(Christianity)

When Jesus lived, many people followed him and listened to him. There were twelve special people who stayed with Jesus and helped him. They were called disciples. The most famous was called Peter. When Jesus had gone to heaven, Peter became the leader of the Church. Peter had a brother who also followed Jesus and also became a disciple. His name was Andrew. Andrew was a fisherman. When Jesus walked up to him and told him to follow him, Andrew, like his brother, put down his fishing nets and stayed with Jesus until Jesus was crucified. He also saw Jesus after he had risen from the dead.

Once Jesus had left them and gone to heaven, Andrew did not stay with the other disciples. Instead he travelled around the Roman Empire telling everyone about the stories Jesus told, his great miracles and that he had risen from the dead.

The Romans believed that their Emperor was a god. When they heard Andrew talking about Jesus they followed him and had him arrested. Andrew continued to tell people about Jesus. The Romans had him crucified like Jesus. But to make his death even slower (it would have taken hours) they tied him to two pieces of diagonal wood. Even when on the cross and dying Andrew was still telling people about Jesus.

After he died his body was taken away for a special burial. Hundreds of years later the person looking after the bones of Andrew, St. Rule, had a dream. In the dream he was told by an angel to take the bones to Scotland. He did so, and built a small church to keep the bones in. People came from all over Scotland to see the bones – at the place now called St. Andrew's. Scottish leaders believed that having these bones helped them in battle. Today in St. Andrew's Cathedral you can see the place where some of these bones are kept.

Because of Andrew's great bravery and devotion to Jesus, the people of Scotland decided to make him their patron (special) saint. Their flag – two white lines, crossing diagonally – became the symbol of St. Andrew and 30th November became the day to celebrate his life.

Follow-up question
Andrew knew Jesus for three years and saw him die and be resurrected.

◆ Why do you think Andrew was prepared to die for Jesus?

Brilliant Stories for Assemblies
© Paul Urry

St. Patrick
(Christianity)

Patrick was born into a poor farming family in France. He was captured by pirates and sold in Ireland. There he lived on the sides of hills, looking after sheep and pigs. Eventually he managed to escape and get back to France. There he listened to the stories about Jesus. One night he had a dream. In the dream the people of Ireland were calling him back to tell them about Jesus. Patrick did not want to go back and ignored the dream. Patrick knew that he was not from an important, educated family but he carried on learning about Jesus. Eventually he was made a priest. Again he had a dream about the people of Ireland calling him. This time he decided to leave France and go back to Ireland, where previously he had been a slave.

When he disembarked from his boat and landed the people of the area thought he was going to steal their things, so they went down to the beach to kill him. The story says that when they saw the peace in his face they immediately threw down their weapons and became Christians.

Patrick travelled all over Ireland converting people to Christianity – something they had never heard of before.

One story tells of an important leader who was trying to understand how God could be three things – God, Jesus and the Holy Spirit. Patrick thought for a minute then bent down to the grass. He picked a small plant and said, 'Look at this shamrock. It has three leaves, but it is still one plant'. The leader knew straight away that Patrick was a wise and holy man.

Patrick stayed in Ireland for thirty years, building churches and preaching to people.

Patrick died on 17th March. This day is now celebrated as the national day of Ireland and people wear shamrocks to show that they are Irish.

Follow-up questions

Patrick chose to return to a place where people had used him as a slave and tried to kill him.

- Why do you think Patrick chose to do this and not stay where he was safe?

Brilliant Stories for Assemblies
© Paul Urry

This page may be photocopied by the purchasing institution only.

33

St. Christopher
(Christianity)

Props suggested
A picture of St. Christopher, or a St. Christopher pendant.

This story is set two hundred years after Jesus lived, in an area known as Turkey today. A huge man lived in that area. It is believed that his name was Ofer. He was strong and tall. He used a thick wooden staff to help him walk. He was taught about Jesus by a hermit and became a Christian. A hermit is someone who chooses to live by themselves away from towns and noise. As Ofer listened to the stories about Jesus he thought carefully about how he could tell others. Should he live like the hermit and wait for others to find him? Should he travel to different towns and speak there? He knew that if you were a Christian at that time you would be arrested and put to death by the Romans, but he still wanted to serve Jesus. After talking to the hermit he decided that he should live a simple life on the shore of a strong river and help people cross the river as there were no bridges there.

Ofer left the hermit and built his own shelter. Every day people would walk up to the shelter and ask for Ofer's help to cross the river. He lifted people up with his huge arms and used his immense strength to cross the river. When people asked why he did this he told them about Jesus.

On one particular night there was a huge storm. Ofer went into his shelter to get away from the wind and rain. Late into the night there was a banging on his door. Ofer could barely hear it over the noise of the storm. As he opened the door he saw a small child. The boy asked if Ofer could help him cross the river. Ofer was surprised and offered the boy some food and a bed for the night, so that they could cross when the weather was better. But the boy said that he must cross that night.

Ofer got his staff and cloak and walked down to the river with the boy.

He lifted the boy onto his shoulder and waded into the cold water with the wind blowing in his face and the rain dripping down his body. As he slowly crossed the river he noticed that the boy was getting heavier and heavier. Still he kept going. As he got to the other side he could only just carry the child. As he put him down on the other side of the river, he saw that the boy had changed into a man. Instantly he realized that this was Jesus and he fell to his knees. After telling Ofer that he had been a good man and had served him well, Jesus disappeared.

Ofer became famous and converted lots of people to Christianity. He was eventually arrested and killed in AD 251. Today he is still remembered as the patron saint of travellers.

Follow-up question
◆ Why might travellers welcome the special protection given by St. Christopher?

This page may be photocopied by the purchasing institution only.

34

Brilliant Stories for Assemblies
© Paul Urry

Abraham and Isaac

(Judaism)

Note: The story can be found in Genesis 22:1–18.

Abraham was a great servant of God. He listened to him and did what God wanted him to do. Abraham had left his town because God had told him that there was a greater place. Because Abraham worshipped God, God made sure that Abraham and his wife, Sarah, had a baby boy, called Isaac. Abraham and Sarah loved Isaac and praised God for him.

As Isaac grew he learned about the greatness of God and listened to his mother and father. One day God asked Abraham to kill an animal for him.

'Yes Lord,' said Abraham. 'What would you like me to sacrifice for you?'

'Take your only son, whom you love, build a fire and kill Isaac there for me.'

Abraham was shocked by what God had asked but he knew that what God wanted was important. Without telling Sarah, he loaded up a donkey with wood and told Isaac that he was to travel to the top of a mountain for a sacrifice to God.

After three days of travelling, they arrived at the top of the mountain. Abraham collected the wood and placed it in a pile.

Isaac looked puzzled. 'Father,' he said, 'I can see the wood and the fire. Where is the animal to be sacrificed?'

Abraham looked sad. 'Believe in God,' he answered. He tied Isaac's hands behind his back, and took out his knife.

Isaac stared at the blade. Abraham lifted the knife up high, looked at his son and was about to plunge the knife into him, when a angel from God called out, 'Abraham! Abraham! Don't touch the boy. God knows that you will do anything for him. Look over in the trees and you will find a sheep. Untie Isaac and sacrifice the sheep instead.'

Abraham walked over to the trees and, just as the angel had said, a sheep was there. He untied Isaac and they both worshipped God there.

The angel from God spoke again to Abraham and Isaac, 'Because of your great faith, your family will live forever in this land. They will have peace and be happy.'

Abraham and Isaac left the mountain and praised God.

Follow-up questions
- Why do you think Abraham was prepared to sacrifice his only son?
- Was God fair with Abraham?

Brilliant Stories for Assemblies
© Paul Urry

This page may be photocopied by the purchasing institution only.

35

The wisdom of Solomon
(Judaism)

Note: The story can be found in 1 Kings 3:16–28.

King Solomon was a great and powerful king of Israel. He built temples and worshipped God. He prayed to God that he might become a wise and good king of his people. God was pleased that Solomon had not asked to be rich or to destroy his enemies, but to be wise. He gave him his wish.

Two women came to see Solomon one day. They were living in the same house and each had a small child.

'Great king,' said the first woman, 'in the night this woman's baby died. She took my son and put hers next to me so that when I woke up I would think that my son had died. But I know my son, and I know that she has him.'

'She is lying!' shouted the second woman, 'She wants to take my son off of me.'

'Please help me,' pleaded the first woman.

King Solomon thought for a minute. The baby could only belong to one of the women, but how was he going to find out? One was lying and one was telling the truth.

Eventually he spoke to one of his servants, 'Bring me my sword. I will cut the baby in half so that you may both share him.'

'No!' shouted the first woman, 'you must not kill the baby. Give the baby to the other woman rather than kill it.'

Solomon turned to the second woman. 'What do you think?' he asked her.

'Cut the baby in half,' she defiantly said, 'then neither of us will have him.'

Solomon smiled. He took the baby in his arms and gave it to the first woman saying, 'You are the true mother of this baby. Only a real mother would rather give her only son away than see him killed.'

The woman thanked the king and went from the great hall. All of Israel heard of how wise Solomon had been and they greatly respected their king.

Follow-up question
Solomon had asked God to make him wise.

◆ Do you think he was right to ask for wisdom or should he have asked for great power or money?

Brilliant Stories for Assemblies
© Paul Urry

Guru Nanak, the founder of Sikhism

(Sikhism)

In 1469, over five hundred years ago, a boy was born in India. His name was Nanak. He was trained by his father to look after the accounts of businesses. However, Nanak spent most of his time thinking. He thought about God. He thought about the Hindus and Muslims who lived and had battles all around the area where he lived. He thought about what they believed in and why they believed it.

As he got older Nanak got married and had two children. But there seemed to be something always on his mind. One day Nanak went down to the river. He walked into it and went under the water. The people there started to worry when he did not come out of the water again. The people of the village searched in the river, but they could not find him. Eventually they gave up and thought that he had drowned.

After three days, however, he reappeared out of the water as if nothing had happened. Everyone was surprised to see him. Nanak said nothing, just walked up the bank of the river. He carried on into the village and said, 'There is no Hindu, no Muslim, just God. I will follow God.' People in the village were either Hindu or Muslim and were very surprised to hear what he said.

He decided that he should tell people about what he had learned. He asked a friend of his who could play a flute to help him tell others. Nanak had his words put into a poem and his friend played a tune to help people remember what he had said.

He travelled hundreds of miles telling people about God. Eventually, as he got older, he stayed in one place. Lots of people stayed with him. Some were old, others young, some rich, others poor. Lots of people liked what he said; they were peaceful people who wanted to find out about God.

There are many stories about the miracles that Nanak performed. Most are about how peaceful and loving Nanak was, caring for everyone around him.

Follow-up questions
◆ Why do you think people listened to Nanak and moved to where he was?
◆ Do you think you would have liked Nanak if you had met him?

Brilliant Stories for Assemblies
© Paul Urry

This page may be photocopied by the purchasing institution only.

37

The birth of the Khalsa
(Sikhism)

Props suggested
Pictures of Guru Gobind Singh and the five Ks.

Sikhism is a peaceful religion. However, there have been times in its history when other people have attacked Sikhs. One such time was in 1699. The Emperor of India was going to attack them. Their leader or guru (which means teacher), whose name was Gobind Singh, called all the Sikhs together at his tent. Thousands arrived to hear what he was going to say. He walked out of his tent in full blue military uniform, his eyes fixed on the crowds. He held his sword high in his hand and spoke clearly to the crowd. 'Who here is prepared to die for their faith? I want the head of a faithful Sikh.' The crowd went silent. Again he called to the people.

Eventually one man, Daya Ram, called out. 'Take my head, great guru. My head has always been yours.'

Daya Ram followed Guru Gobind Singh into his tent. The crowd listened. They heard a swishing sound of a sword moving through the air and a thud on the ground. Gobind Singh came back out of the tent with his sword dripping with blood. Again he called to the crowd demanding another head. Another man stepped forward. They went into the tent. Again they heard the sound of the sword and the thud on the ground.

As Gobind Singh came out he saw that many people had left, scared that he was going to kill them all. He called three more times for the head of a faithful Sikh. Again, three more times, a Sikh came forward, went into the tent only for the Guru to come out with blood dripping from his sword.

After he came out of the tent for the fifth time looked slowly around the crowd and went into the tent by himself. He came out again with all five men alive. They were all wearing golden uniforms and carrying swords.

The guru spoke to the crowd. He said that these brave Sikhs were going to be the first five members of the Khalsa – an army for God – in which everyone was equal. Everyone cheered the five.

That day everyone in the crowd had taken part in the ceremony and become members of the Khalsa themselves.

To show that they were faithful Sikhs, Gobind Singh told people to wear the five Ks

Note: The five K's are called such because in Punjabi all their names begin with the sound 'K':

- Kesh — Uncut hair
- Kangha — Small wooden comb
- Kachs — A special Sikh type of underwear
- Kara — Steel bangle
- Kirpan — Short sword

Follow-up questions
The first five showed great faith and bravery in their leader.

- How do you think the men felt as they were going into the tent?
- Why do you think they did it?

Brilliant Stories for Assemblies
© Paul Urry

The Buddha and the mustard seed

(Buddhism)

A young woman had an only son, who died. In her grief she carried him to all of her neighbours asking for help. 'Why is she doing this?' they asked each other. 'Can't she see that he is dead?' However, one neighbour said that although he could not give her medicine he knew of one person who might be able to help, the Buddha.

The young woman ran through the streets until she came to the Buddha, asking him if he would help her. He replied, 'Go to every house and ask for some mustard seeds. But you cannot take them from any house where someone has died.'

The woman ran quickly to the first house.

'Have you any mustards seeds?' she asked.

'Yes,' said the man.

'Has anyone in your family died that you know?' she asked, as the man gave her the mustard seeds.

'Of course. I have lost a lot of my family. I am an old man and have seen a lot of sorrow. Please do not remind me of these things.'

Remembering what the Buddha had said, she gave the mustard seeds back to the man and said thank you.

The young woman went from house to house asking the same question. Lots of people had mustard seeds but they all knew people in their family that had died.

Eventually the woman realized what was happening.

'I have been a selfish fool,' she said to herself. 'Everyone dies. I know I cannot bring my son back.' She returned to the Buddha and said thank you for helping her understand these things.

She stayed with the Buddha and listened to his teachings. She learned that in life there are many things that make you sad and suffer, but that there are also things that make you happy and cheerful.

Follow-up questions
◆ Can you think of one time in your life when you were unhappy? Remember how people helped you.
◆ Now can you think of one time when you were really happy?

Brilliant Stories for Assemblies
© Paul Urry

This page may be photocopied by the purchasing institution only.

39

The Buddha cares for a sick man
(Buddhism)

On one of his many travels, the Buddha was invited into a place for sick people for something to eat. As he looked into the rooms he saw many unwell people being looked after. However, there was one particular sick man that no one was looking after. He lay on the ground with dirt and mud around him and on his clothes. He was not moving and was surprised when the Buddha came into his room. The Buddha asked him why, if he was so ill, no one was caring for him.

The man replied that when he had been healthy he had never looked after ill people, so now that he was sick no one was going to look after him.

The Buddha wanted to help. He said, 'I will help you,' and he went over and picked him up. He cleaned the man's hair and face. He took off the dirty and smelly clothes that the man had been wearing for a long time and helped the man get into clean clothes. The people around watched this great man, respected by everyone, get dirty, whilst helping the man get clean. He got a new mat for the man and sat the man down. He became instantly better. Everyone around saw the miracle that the Buddha had performed.

The man knew how great the Buddha was. *The Buddha is kind and has great spiritual powers. When he picked me up the pain disappeared from my body and I felt immediately calm,* he thought to himself. He said to the Buddha that he would listen to him and tell others about his teaching.

Follow-up questions

There are many stories in which the Buddha cures people and cares for others.

◆ Would you have picked up someone as dirty and ill as the man was?
◆ Why do you think that the Buddha helped the man?

Brilliant Stories for Assemblies
© Paul Urry

Mohammed is called to be a prophet

(Islam)

Note: Explain that there are no pictures of Mohammed as there are for Jesus because you cannot show people in Islamic art.

Mohammed was born in Mecca, Saudi Arabia, in AD 570. He travelled to many countries selling things with his family. Mohammed was a good and kind man who helped solve people's arguments. However, as he travelled, he saw that the people in his country were involved in battles. They also kidnapped people and stole from their neighbours. This greatly upset Mohammed and he spent a lot of his time thinking. To help him think, Mohammed used to go to a cave high up on a mountain, sometimes by himself, sometimes with his family.

He often stayed thinking in the cave all night. On one particular night, when he was all alone, the angel Gabriel appeared to him and said, 'Read'

But Mohammed said, 'I cannot read'.

The angel again said, 'Read'.

Mohammed again said he could not and the angel disappeared. Mohammed went back down the mountain to his wife and told her what had happened. She was overjoyed that Allah (God) had sent an angel to visit Mohammed. But he was not so sure. He worried about what it all meant.

Later he went back to the mountain and Gabriel again visited him. Mohammed now knew that he was to be a prophet for Allah.

Few people, however, believed what he said and, after three years, he had only thirty followers. At that time people believed in lots of gods and thought the idea of just one, all-powerful god was wrong.

But it was to get even worse for Mohammed. Not only did people not believe him, but they started to threaten him and his family, and made him leave Mecca. Mohammed did not stop telling people about Allah though. He did not threaten people but peacefully explained what God had told him through Gabriel.

Mohammed's life began to change when leaders started to listen to him. They understood what he said and helped him change people's minds. Mohammed wanted to pray in Mecca at the holiest site. The people of the city stopped him doing it. Mohammed and his followers came back and kept trying. Again the people of Mecca stopped him.

All the time Mohammed believed he was the messenger of God and spoke to people who would listen. He would tell them about the greatness of God and also how God wanted them to live their lives.

As Mohammed grew older, more and more people started to follow his teachings. Today Islam, the faith of Muslims, is one of the largest religions in the world. We know about Mohammed and his life through the Quran, the Islamic holy book.

Follow-up questions

- Have you ever thought that you were right about something and people did not listen? How did it make you feel?
- How did people react when you told them?

Brilliant Stories for Assemblies
© Paul Urry

This page may be photocopied by the purchasing institution only.

41

Mohammed's night-time journey

(Islam)

One night Mohammed was fast asleep in Mecca. Suddenly, he was woken up by a bright light. In front of him was the angel Gabriel and a strange creature that was brilliantly white. It was the size of a donkey, but had the head of a woman and the tail of a peacock.

The prophet was told to get onto the back of this animal and they rode out into the night. Travelling at great speed, they came to Jerusalem. When the prophet got off he a saw a golden ladder that rose up to heaven.

As the prophet and Gabriel climbed, they passed into the first heaven. There he saw Adam, the first person created by God.

He climbed further. In the second heaven he saw Abraham, who always listened to God, and in the third heaven, there was Joseph, famous for his coat of many colours.

The prophet continued climbing, to the fourth, fifth and sixth heavens, where he saw other great prophets of God.

Finally, at the gate of the seventh heaven, he met Jesus. He asked Jesus to introduce him to God, which Jesus did. God told Mohammed that people should pray to him five times a day.

After speaking to God, Mohammed descended the ladder back down to earth. The place he put his foot down was a rock in Jerusalem. He climbed back onto the animal again and quickly travelled back to Mecca, all in the same night (an amazing total of one thousand, six hundred miles).

The following morning, when he woke up, the people did not believe him. 'If you travelled that far you must have seen people.'

'Of course I did,' said Mohammed. 'There was a group of travellers just outside the city. Their camel ran away. That was the first thing I saw.'

So the people left Mecca and found the group of travellers. They asked about the night before: yes, one of their camels did run off and, yes, they did see a fantastic animal. Everyone there believed Mohammed and began to worship God.

Today, the place where Mohammed's foot stepped on the rock is a very special place for Muslims. It is high up in the centre of the city. To protect the place, a big mosque was built around it. The top of the mosque is covered with gold to make it shine out. When you go into the mosque – called the Dome of the Rock – you can see in the centre the rock surrounded by a cage. In one corner of the cage there is a box. To touch the place where Mohammed came back from heaven you have to put your whole arm into the darkness and there you can feel a hollow in the rock.

Follow-up questions
◆ Why did people not believe Mohammed?
◆ Why did Mohammed see only certain people when he went into heaven?

Brilliant Stories for Assemblies
© Paul Urry

Rama and Sita
(Hinduism)

There was once a great prince called Rama. Everyone loved Rama. He was a kind prince who was handsome, good at hunting and a great soldier. When he was old enough to marry he met a young princess called Sita and immediately fell in love with her. They were married and lived happily together for twelve years.

As Rama's father grew older, he decided to choose who would be king when he died. Rama was chosen, although he was not the eldest son. Everyone was happy with this, except the mother of the eldest son. She made sure that Rama was forced to leave the city for seven years. Sita wanted to go with him and also one of his brothers, Lakshmana. Everyone cried as they left the city together to go and live in the forest. Rama promised that he would be back to be their king. Rama's father was so upset that he would continue to cry out Rama's name until he died.

An evil king, Ravana, out hunting one day saw the beautiful Sita and wanted her for his wife. He saw that there were two men with her and thought of a way to take her. He commanded a spirit to change into a beautiful deer. On seeing the deer Rama and Lakshmana decided to hunt it. They made a circle in the ground and told Sita that she would be safe as long as she stayed in the circle.

The two men started to follow the deer deeper and deeper into the forest. As soon as they had gone Ravana appeared to Sita. He pretended to be ill and asked for help. Sita, being a kind person, stepped out of the circle to help the old man, who instantly changed into Ravana and took her away.

When Rama returned he was devastated. He had lost his beautiful wife. Then he heard a cry. He walked over and saw an eagle on the ground.

'I saw Ravana take Sita,' he said. 'I tried to attack him but they cut my wings.'

Rama and Lakshmana started their journey to get Sita back. As they travelled, people who wanted to help Rama joined his army. Even the great monkey god, Hanuman, joined them.

There was a great battle at Ravana's palace. Rama was brave and fought his way to where Sita was being held. His army defeated Ravana and they returned to the forest.

When seven years had passed. Rama, Sita and Lakshmana returned home to a great celebration. People cheered and clapped and lit special candles, divas, which they placed on rivers and walls. Every year, during Divali, the story of good defeating evil is celebrated by the lighting of divas.

Follow-up questions
◆ What do you like best about Rama?
◆ Are you like Rama in any ways?

Brilliant Stories for Assemblies
© Paul Urry

This page may be photocopied by the purchasing institution only.

43

Ganesh
(Hinduism)

Props suggested
Pictures of Ganesh, and possibly Shiva and Parvati.

One of the most popular gods in Hinduism is Ganesh. He is always present at Hindu weddings and is a symbol of good luck. However, there is one unusual thing about him ... his head. This story tells you how he got it.

One day, when the great god Shiva had gone on a journey, his wife, Parvati, decided to have a bath. So that no one would disturb her, she created a model of a boy and breathed air into it. Instantly the boy came alive. She called him Ganesh.

'Make sure that no one comes down to the river,' she told him.

Ganesh stood at the entrance to the path down to the river and waited. On his return Shiva saw this strange boy barring his way down to the river.

'Let me pass,' demanded Shiva.

'I cannot let anyone pass,' said Ganesh, not knowing who Shiva was.

Shiva was so furious that he drew his sword and cut off the boy's head with one swift blow.

Parvati heard the noise and came to see what was going on.

'What have you done Shiva?' she cried, as she saw Ganesh lying on the floor dead.

When Shiva realized that he had killed their son he was very upset.

'What can I do to make things right again?' he asked.

'Send your servants into the woods to fetch the head of anyone sleeping, whose head is facing north.' Parvati answered.

So Shiva sent out his servants. As they wandered through the trees, they came to a clearing. Lying on the ground was a small elephant asleep. They checked and his head was facing north. Thinking they needed the head of any living creature they cut it off and returned to Shiva and Parvati.

Parvati was upset that they had not brought back a boy's head, but Shiva placed the elephant head on the boy and breathed life into him. Shiva was sad that Parvati was still not happy and so he granted Ganesh the power to answer people's prayers.

Follow-up question
Shiva cut the boy's head off without thinking.

◆   What have you done that you have later known was wrong?

Brilliant Stories for Assemblies
© Paul Urry

Racism
(Children)

Geena stood nervously by the school gate, holding her mother's hand tightly. It was her first day at her new school. Her new teacher came out into the playground and told her where to line up. She waved to her mum and went into school. The teacher told her where to sit and Geena started working.

Geena loved school. She listened carefully to the teacher and worked quickly and quietly. If someone on her table could not do a question, Geena helped them. Everyone on her table spoke to Geena, welcomed her to their school and smiled at her. Except one, Emma.

At playtime Geena's teacher asked who was going to play with her. Lots of hands went up. Emma's did not.

Geena had a great day until, in the afternoon, she asked Emma to pass a pencil. Emma ignored her. She asked again. Emma did not even look at her. Geena wasn't sure what she had done, but she still went home happy.

The next day Emma was the same with Geena. Friends on their table asked Emma what the problem was. Emma stared at them and said, 'It's obvious isn't it? I don't know why you want to be her friend.' The other children looked at each other, puzzled.

This went on for the rest of the week. By Friday Geena was fed up with it.

'Would you like to skip?' Geena asked Emma at play. Emma ignored her again. 'We can't carry on like this. Why won't you talk to me?' For the first time Emma turned around and looked at Geena.

'Why should I? Look at you!'

'What do you mean?' asked Geena.

'You're dirty!'

'No, I'm not!' Geena said firmly.

'Then why is your skin brown?'

Geena was stunned. She had never met anyone who did not like her because she was Asian.

(The story can end here for a discussion and suggestions on what Geena, her friends and the teacher could do. The suggested ending below focuses on ignorance.)

'My mum said that because I have had a good first week I could invite someone round my house to eat tonight. Would you like to come?' Geena asked.

Emma was surprised. She expected Geena to be cross. 'I'll think about it,' she said.

That afternoon Emma kept looking up from her work and staring at Geena. After school she ran up to her dad. Geena could not hear what they were saying, but her dad smiled and nodded. Emma looked round and ran up to Geena.

'Can I come round then?' she asked

Geena was overjoyed. 'Of course,' she said.

(continued on next page)

When they arrived, Emma had a shock. Geena's mum's clothes were very different from her own mum's and she wore fantastic jewellery and make up. Emma had never seen anything like it before. She stared at Geena's mum, who kindly smiled back.

Follow-up questions

- Why did Emma react the way she did?
- Why do you think she changed her mind?
- Was she right to change her mind?

Brilliant Stories for Assemblies
© Paul Urry

Racism
(Parents)

'Please, Mum!' Daniel pleaded for the thousandth time.

'OK! If you stop asking me! What's his name anyway?' she asked.

'He's called Bil and he is a great mate,' he shouted, grabbing his bag and running off to school with a smile on his face. Straight away he ran up to Bilal, his new best friend. 'You can come round to my house tonight, my mum said it's OK.'

'Great! We can play on your new computer game.' It was all the boys talked about all day!

At the end of school they ran off together down the street, laughing and joking. At Daniel's front door he rang the bell. His mum opened the door, looked outside and half closed it.

'What are your doing, Daniel?' she said.

'You said I could bring a friend to tea tonight, mum. This is Bil.'

'Oh … right … sorry … um, I forgot, yes that's it. I forgot. I'm just on my way to the shops. It will have to be another day.'

'You never go to the shops at this time,' Daniel said, a little shocked.

'But today I have to,' she said firmly.

Bil looked at Daniel, 'Another day then.' Daniel nodded and went into the house. His mum carried on washing up.

'I thought you were going shopping,' he said angrily.

'I think we're OK now,' she replied quietly.

Daniel went to his room.

Back at Bil's house, his mum was surprised. 'Why are you here, Bilal? I thought you were round at Daniel's.' Bilal told his mum what had happened. She nodded knowingly.

The next week it was Daniel and Bilal's class assembly. They were very excited. Lots of parents had come to see it. Daniel stood up and told everyone about his science work.

'He's very good,' Bilal's mum said, leaning forward to speak to Daniel's parents.

'Yes, we're very proud of him.' they said turning round. They stopped when they saw who was talking.

'That's my son, Bilal, but he likes to be called Bil. They're great friends. They help each other and are so happy together.'

'I know,' Daniel's mum sighed.

After the assembly, the boys ran up to their parents. 'Bilal's mum has invited me round to tea tonight. Can I go?'

Daniel's parents glanced at each other. Without looking at Bilal or his mum they quietly said, 'OK'.

The boys ran off smiling back to their teacher. But Daniel's parents walked off without saying anything.

Follow-up questions
- Why do you think Daniel's parents reacted the way they did?
- How could they change their minds, do you think?

This page may be photocopied by the purchasing institution only.

Disability
(Hearing)

'Gary! Will you stop daydreaming and listen?' shouted his teacher.

Gary just stared back. He was a popular person in class, great at football and funny, but he kept getting into trouble. His friends tried to help him but he would not listen.

Gary started his work. He carefully wrote the date and then stopped.

'What's wrong?' Liam asked but Gary did not answer. Liam nudged him.

'What's wrong?' he asked again.

Gary looked straight at Liam. 'I don't know what to do.'

'Why? Miss has explained what to do.'

'I don't know.'

Gary kept quiet as usual and managed to copy some of Liam's work. That usually stopped him getting into more trouble.

That afternoon on the way home from school something terrible happened. An unhappy Gary was walking ahead of Liam. He stepped up to the road and started to walk across.

'GARY!!!!' Liam screamed, 'LOOK OUT!!!' Gary did nothing. At the last minute he turned and saw a car coming towards him. He tried to move out of the way. The driver managed to swerve but still hit Gary's leg. He spun around and fell heavily to the ground.

Liam and some other friends ran up. Gary was lying on the ground. The driver jumped out of his car and ran up too, saying, 'I didn't see him.' He started to shake but called an ambulance on his phone. Liam ran to Gary's house to tell his parents.

When Gary woke up in hospital he saw his leg in plaster. He wondered how he had got there. His mum was crying and his dad was holding her. He tried to smile, but it hurt him. They held his hand. His mum carried on crying.

After several days he was allowed out of hospital and Liam called round to see him.

'Can I see Gary, please?' he asked.

'Of course. Come in, Liam.'

Liam looked at Gary's crutches and broken leg. 'Why didn't you move when I called?' he asked.

'Did you call?'

'Are you kidding? I shouted!'

'I didn't hear you,' he said, looking straight at Liam.

'You must have done. Everyone else looked round.'

The friends looked at each other. After a while Gary carried on. 'I've been thinking. I didn't hear the car either.'

'Have you told your parents?' asked Liam.

'Not yet. I can't hear you all the time. I've known for a long time in school that I couldn't hear the teacher. That's why I don't always know what to do. I'm not stupid, you know!'

(continued on next page)

Brilliant Stories for Assemblies
© Paul Urry

'I know that,' Liam said reassuringly.

Gary did tell his parents and they took him to the doctor's. After a few weeks he had a hearing aid and noticed things he had never known about before – the birds singing in the trees, the laughter in the playground and the sound of the traffic on the roads. He was also much happier in school.

'Gary! Will you stop daydreaming and listen?' shouted his teacher. Gary smiled. He *had* been daydreaming this time.

'No need to shout, Miss,' he said, and everyone laughed.

Follow-up question
◆ Why was Liam such a good friend?

Brilliant Stories for Assemblies
© Paul Urry

This page may be photocopied by the purchasing institution only.

49

Disability
(Visual)

It was a lazy Saturday. Chloe and Haydon were walking down the High Street, bored.

'I'm fed up,' Chloe said. 'There's nothing to do and we haven't got any money.'

'I know,' Haydon added, kicking stones as they went down the road.

Walking up to a zebra crossing, Haydon and Chloe waited for the traffic to stop. Haydon looked down.

'Why have they put these silly bubbly things in the pavement? They hurt my feet,' he said.

'Yeah, they're annoying,' Chloe replied.

Just then an old man came to stand by the crossing with them. They stared at him. In one hand he had a white stick and was tapping the ground with it and, in the other hand, he had a dog on a special lead.

Haydon nudged Chloe and smiled. As the traffic stopped they started to cross the road. The man and the dog followed. Haydon started to walk into the dog, forcing the man towards the stationary cars. With the side of her foot Chloe joined in nudging the dog. Accidentally she stepped on the dog's paw. It let out a yelp and moved suddenly back. The old man wasn't ready and tumbled backwards, hitting the bonnet of a car as he fell heavily on the road.

Chloe and Haydon looked at each other and started to run. They had got to the other side of the road but a man and woman, who had seen what had happened, stopped them. Chloe and Haydon looked around. Everyone was watching them – people in cars, in shop windows and on the pavement.

Note: What should they do? Should they talk to the man and woman, even though they were strangers? One possible ending follows …

The man and woman stood in front of them, stopping Chloe and Haydon from going anywhere. A lady had got out of one of the cars and was talking to the old man. She carefully helped him up and over to the other side of the road. She sat him down on a nearby bench and after making sure he was all right, she returned to her car and slowly drove off, staring at the children. Haydon and Chloe looked at each other. They were relieved the man was not seriously hurt. They slowly walked up to him, with everyone still watching them.

'Um … s … s … sorry,' Chloe eventually mumbled.

The old man said nothing. He was holding on to his leg. They looked up and saw a small boy with his mum pointing at them.

'Are you OK?' Haydon asked.

'I have been better. Why did you do it?'

'I don't know. It seemed funny,' Haydon said.

'Are you totally blind?' Chloe asked.

'Yes, and I have been for the past ten years. I knew what it was like to see all the things you can, but now I need Tara, my dog, and this stick.'

After making sure the man was OK they apologized again and walked away.

Follow-up questions
- How do you think Chloe and Haydon felt?
- Should they have spoken to the man even though he was was a stranger?

Brilliant Stories for Assemblies
© Paul Urry

Disability
(Physical)

'Race you to school,' James dared.

'Why, when you always lose?' Stacey laughed.

'We'll see this time,' James said, running off down the street.

Stacey finished putting on her coat and, closing the door, chased after James. Stacey was the best runner in the school and was quickly catching up with James.

'You're so slow,' Stacey called. James looked over his shoulder to see where Stacey was. She was getting closer and closer. James was trying really hard to run as quickly as he could. Looking over his shoulder again he knew he was going to be caught. Turning the last corner, he looked back again. Suddenly he went flying through the air. He landed heavily and felt a huge pain in his leg.

'Arghhh!' James cried, holding onto his leg.

As Stacey turned the corner she saw what had happened. Lying on the floor were two people. She went over to James and tried to help him up.

'Leave him alone,' the other person said. 'He has broken his leg. I heard it snap. Could you help me first, please?'

Stacey looked over. Next to the young man was a wheelchair.

'Get yourself up. I'm here for my friend.'

The man pulled out his phone and rang for an ambulance. James lay in agony on the floor.

By the time the ambulance had arrived, the man had pulled himself back up into his wheelchair and was talking to some police officers. Stacey stayed with James, a large crowd of children and parents were watching.

After school Stacey's dad took her to the hospital to see James. He lay on the bed, his leg in plaster. There were scratches and bruises on his face and arms. He looked bad.

'How are you feeling?' she asked.

'It hurts so much. The doctors have said that I need to stay in for a couple of days, but then I can go home with some crutches.'

Stacey and her dad walked quietly out of the ward and down the corridor. They stepped into the lift and heard a voice behind them.

'Could you hold the door open while I get in?'

'No, why shou ... ' Stacey stopped speaking as she turned around. It was the man in the wheelchair again.

'How's your friend?' the young man asked.

'Um, he's ... um ... fine.' She paused. 'Thank you for getting an ambulance. I didn't know what to do. Dad, this is the man who helped James.'

'Thank you,' Stacey's dad said. 'James and his parents are in the next ward. I'm sure they would like to see you.'

'I might do, I am visiting a friend there.' He turned to Stacey. 'I'm glad he's well. He is going to find it tough with crutches. He will need your help. But can I ask you a question? Why didn't you help me?'

Follow-up question
◆ Why didn't Stacey help?

Fighting
(Between schools)

It was a beautiful spring day. The sun shone down and blossom was growing on the trees. Even better, school had finished for the day and Louise and Jonny were chatting about what to do.

'Let's go to the park. It's such a nice day. We can relax there,' said Louise.

Jonny agreed and the two of them went straight to the park. Suddenly, both were knocked to the ground from behind. Before Jonny could turn around he felt a kick in his ribs. Somebody else trod on Louise's hand. As they looked up, they saw three children running away.

Slowly, they got to their feet.

'You OK?' Jonny asked.

'Yeah,' Louise answered. Why did they attack us?'

Louise's mum asked the same question when she got home.

'I don't know,' Louise protested.

'You must have been doing something wrong.'

'We weren't! We had only gone to the park.'

Next day at school they told their friends. It seemed strange. No one even knew the children.

'Anyway,' Louise said, 'I think they were from a different school.'

At playtime, Jonny approached some children who usually played together in a group. They talked secretly together in a corner of the playground.

That night Jonny and Louise went straight home. A couple more days passed.

The next day they had a special assembly. All the children sat waiting in silence. The headteacher looked worried and cross.

'Last night,' she began, 'two Year Three children were shouted at by three pupils from another school. They sensibly ignored them and carried on walking. However, the other children started to chase them and push them around. This is a serious and worrying incident. I understand from the teachers that this has happened before.'

Louise nervously looked around the hall but could not see Jonny.

(continued on next page)

Brilliant Stories for Assemblies
© Paul Urry

'However,' she continued, 'things got much worse. A group of children from OUR school ran across and rather than helping the children on the ground, started fighting with the aggressive children.'

There was a stunned silence. Some children started to look around the hall.

'The police were called and took the children back to their schools. I have spoken to the headteacher from the other school and he is as worried about these incidents as I'm sure you are. I have spoken to all the parents of the children involved.'

She went across to the door and opened it. In walked a group of children with their heads bowed low ... including Jonny.

'I have asked them why they did this. The only answer they gave was because the children were from another school.' She raised her voice, 'NOT because they weren't friends, NOT because they did something wrong, NOT even because they had annoyed them – but just because they wore a different uniform.'

Follow-up questions
- Why didn't Jonny and the other children help the Year 3 children who had been knocked down?
- What should the headteacher do?
- How would Louise have felt seeing Jonny there?

Brilliant Stories for Assemblies
© Paul Urry

This page may be photocopied by the purchasing institution only.

53

Fighting
(Between friends)

Chelsea and Sophie had been best friends since nursery. They enjoyed playing and chatting and liked the same things. They worked hard at school and were always smiling. Their classmates sometimes called them twins because they were always together.

In Year Five they went away for an activity week with the school. They stayed in the same room and talked all night. 'You must run out of things to talk about,' their friends used to joke.

Chelsea and Sophie had a great time away together.

When they returned to school something had changed. A new girl had started. Her name was Natalie.

When Sophie went home that night she saw that Natalie had moved in just two doors away from her. That evening, there was a knock on Sophie's door. 'Do you want to come out and play?' Natalie asked.

'OK,' Sophie replied.

They went to the swings in the park and chatted. They talked about where Natalie had come from and found that they had a lot in common. Only when it began to get dark did they go home.

Next day at school, their class went out to play. Natalie rushed up to Sophie and started talking. As Chelsea came out she saw the two of them talking and walked up to them. 'Hi!' said Chelsea.

Natalie turned her back on Chelsea and carried on talking to Sophie.

'Excuse me!' Chelsea interrupted, 'I want to talk to my friend.'

'Well, I'm talking to MY friend.' Natalie said rudely. She took hold of Sophie and walked her across the playground. Sophie looked helplessly back at Chelsea.

Chelsea just stood there. This had never happened before. And it was the same thing at lunchtime.

After school Natalie called round at Sophie's. 'Coming out?' she asked forcibly.

'I … I'm not sure,' Sophie stuttered.

'Come on!' Natalie demanded.

They walked to the park. There was silence. As before they sat on the swings. Eventually Sophie said, 'You were rude to my best friend today.'

'You don't need her … you've got ME!'

'I do,' Sophie said quietly. 'Chelsea is a great friend and …' she paused thinking that Natalie might get angry, '… I like you … but I have got to be friends with her.'

There was a pause as Natalie thought. 'I really miss my friends in my last school,' she said eventually. 'I want to have nice friends like you.'

'Couldn't all three of us be friends? Chelsea is great,' Sophie said.

The girls walked back home quietly.

(continued on next page)

Brilliant Stories for Assemblies
© Paul Urry

Next day in school Sophie rushed up to Chelsea. 'I phoned you last night but you were out.'

Just then Natalie came up to them. 'Can we be friends please?' she asked Chelsea.

Follow-up questions

◆ What should Natalie do?
◆ Have you ever been in Sophie's position?
◆ How did it make you feel?

Brilliant Stories for Assemblies
© Paul Urry

This page may be photocopied by the purchasing institution only.

55

Stealing
(From friends)

Adnan was a hard-working and friendly member of the class. He loved to help others, was good at cricket and was always cheerful. His teachers would often say – one of the nicest things they could say about any child – that Adnan was simply a pleasure to teach.

On one particular Monday morning he walked into the playground with an even bigger smile on his face than usual. His friends came up to him and he showed them why he was smiling – he had a new coat. Everyone knew that Adnan's family did not have much money and usually he had hand-me-down clothes from his older brothers, but this was the first coat bought just for him!

In class, everyone was making a fuss about Adnan and his coat. Lee sat back and, as he watched, he thought, *It's only a coat. What's the big deal?*

The teacher joined in the fun by calling Adnan's coat for the register. Everyone laughed, but Lee had had enough.

During the afternoon, Lee asked to go to the toilet. He left the room and, picking up Adnan's coat, hid it in the top of a cupboard. He walked quickly back to class, smiling.

At the end of the day, everyone went out of the class with their reading books and got their coats. Adnan looked around for his but could not see it. He asked some of his friends. They looked all around. His teacher told him to look on other classes' coat racks, but he could not find it. He was devastated.

Back at home Adnan's mum was furious, because the coat had cost so much money. She sent Adnan to bed early.

The next day, his teacher asked everyone to look around for the coat. All morning the children thought about where it could be. Lee started to feel guilty.

By the middle of the afternoon Lee had had enough. He asked to go the toilet and, getting the coat from the cupboard, hid it again, this time behind a radiator outside the classroom.

At the end of the day the children got their coats. With others watching, Lee walked up to the radiator and looked behind it.

'Miss, I think I can see something,' he called.

They all went over and pulled the coat out.

'It's my coat!' shouted Adnan. 'Thank you, Lee, you're a real friend.'

'I thought I looked there yesterday,' Arfan said to himself.

Everyone came up to Lee and congratulated him. He felt awful.

The next day, people were still talking about Lee and the coat. At playtime, Lee walked up to Arfan. 'You know I hid the coat, don't you, Arfan?'

Arfan nodded.

'I was just fed up with people going on about it all the time.'

'What should I do, Arfan?' Lee asked.

Follow-up question
◆ What should Lee do?

Brilliant Stories for Assemblies
© Paul Urry

Stealing
(From school)

It had started one Friday. At the end of the day, the teacher was asking his class what they were doing that weekend.

'I'm going to the cinema,' said Tom.

'My mum and dad are taking me shopping. I'm going to get a new dress for a party,' added Maheen.

Jason sat quietly. He did not want to put his hand up or say anything. He knew that he was going to stay in, doing nothing except watching TV. He might go and see if anyone was playing on his street, but he knew that he was not going to go anywhere exciting. His dad had been injured at work and his mum only had a part-time job, so there was not a lot of money to spend on him. But his mum and dad loved him.

He sat and listened to all the things other people were going to get. Jason sat miserably at his desk, looking around his classroom. He enjoyed everything about school, his friends, the playtimes, but especially his work.

As the class lined up to go home, Jason stayed at the back of the line. Everyone went out but he stayed behind. No one was there. He quickly grabbed some pencils and paper, put them in his bag and walked out. It was so easy.

That weekend he had a fantastic time, drawing, colouring and writing. As the days went by he started to take other things. First it was a sharpener and a rubber. Then more paper and rulers, felt-tip pens and even a dictionary. It was always so simple.

No one ever saw him. *Anyway, I'm not hurting anyone*, he used to think.

Jason's class was really excited one day. Their teacher had been reading a fantastic book.

Everyone was captivated by its clever plot. They were all trying to guess the ending, but 'No time left, I'm afraid,' their teacher said. 'I'll read the last chapter tomorrow.'

'Awwwuh,' everyone moaned. They went to line up, all trying to think how it was going to end. Jason was desperate to find out what was going to happen.

'I've got the book at home,' Tom said. 'I'm going to have to read it and find out.'

As the class left, Jason stayed back. From the doorway, Daniel, who had come back to get his lunch box, saw Jason pick up the book and put it his bag. Before Jason could see him, Daniel left the room.

It was late when Jason finished the book and he quickly fell asleep. The book dropped to the floor.

'You're going to be late, Jason,' his mum shouted the next morning. Jason got up dressed and ran to school, leaving the book on the floor.

His teacher looked worried. 'I'm sorry class,' he apologised. 'I've looked everywhere for the book, but I cannot find it.' Daniel looked at Jason.

At playtime, Daniel went up to Jason. 'I saw you take it,' he said. 'You need to tell the teacher.'

Jason was horrified. No one had caught him before. He did not know what to say.

Follow-up questions
- What should Daniel and Jason do?
- Was Jason right to steal?

Brilliant Stories for Assemblies
© Paul Urry

This page may be photocopied by the purchasing institution only.

57

Family
(Helping with new babies)

Hannah was really excited. Her mum and dad had just shown her a very special photograph. They had been to the hospital and a machine had taken a picture of her baby sister still inside her mum! She could see the head, arms and even the fingers. She thought it was wonderful. She was going to be a big sister!

A few months later, Hannah's mum went into hospital. Her dad took her to see her baby sister.

'Hello, Hannah,' said her mum. 'Meet Emily. She's been waiting to see you.'

Hannah looked into the cot and saw Emily fast asleep. *This is the best day of my life,* she thought.

Hannah went into school and told everyone about her new sister. She was so excited. She drew pictures of Emily and wrote stories about how they were going to play together.

But when Emily and her mum came home, things started to change.

First, Hannah held Emily on her shoulder. It felt warm on her back and when she looked Emily had been sick all down her top!

Then there was night-time. Emily seemed to sleep all day but at night she cried and cried. Hannah tried everything to stay asleep but, for a little girl, Emily had a very loud scream! Hannah used to go to school tired.

She wanted to help. One time she lay Emily down and, with her dad watching, she carefully took off her nappy. When Hannah looked at it, it made her feel sick. She ran from the room. Her dad laughed.

But by far the worst thing was her mum and dad spending all their time with Emily.

'Can you listen to me read tonight,' Emily would ask.

'Not tonight,' her exhausted dad would say.

'Mum, can we bake?'

'Another time, dear,' she would say.

From the baby monitor came the sound of Emily waking, and then the crying would start. Hannah was very sad. She did not want her sister now. She had thought it would be fun. At school, she did not talk about Emily any more.

One day, she was watching TV when her mum came into the room holding Emily. Hannah ignored them.

'Hannah,' her mum said, 'would you like a hold?'

'Not really.'

Mum put Emily on Hannah's knee. Hannah held Emily's head carefully and looked down. She stared at Emily and Emily smiled at her.

'I think she likes her big sister,' Mum said.

Hannah thought for a while. 'I think I like her as well.'

'Would you like to feed her?' Mum asked.

(continued on next page)

Brilliant Stories for Assemblies
© Paul Urry

Hannah nodded and went to the kitchen with her Mum and Emily. She put some food on the spoon and gave it to Emily. Emily held the spoon and threw it all over Hannah and laughed.

Hannah's mum looked worried.

'She's quite funny really… for a baby sister,' Hannah laughed.

Follow-up questions
◆ Was Hannah being selfish?
◆ What do you think is the best thing about a baby brother or sister?

Brilliant Stories for Assemblies
© Paul Urry

This page may be photocopied by the purchasing institution only.

59

Family
(Helping each other)

Gary was fed up. He had been happily playing football with his friends at lunchtime when he was called away.

'Gary, you need to come and have your lunch now. Your brother is messing about.'

As much as Gary was fed up with this, he was used to it. His brother was ill. It meant that he sometimes shouted out or threw things.

Everyone knew what Paul was like – that he went to hospital for tests, and all the tablets he had to take – but he was OK most of the time.

When he was causing problems, however, there was only one person who could help him – his brother Gary.

Gary walked to the front of the dinner queue, got his food and sat next to Paul.

'What's up now?' he asked Paul.

Paul was sitting on the floor, with his plate in front of him. Some of the younger children were pointing and laughing.

'Come on,' Gary said, 'put your plate on the table.'

Slowly, Paul stood up. He put some beans on his fork and flicked them at Gary. They hit him in the face. Everyone on the table stopped eating and talking and stared.

Gary calmly wiped them off as Paul sat down. Although all of Gary's friends had seen this before, they were always amazed at how calm he was.

'I would've hit him for that,' one friend said to another.

'I know, but I couldn't be bothered.' was the quiet reply.

After lunch, they went out to play. Gary stayed close to Paul, watching his friends playing and having a good time.

'Do you fancy coming to the park after school?' Kira asked Gary.

'Can't tonight,' he sighed. 'I have to walk Paul home. I can get there later.'

'I'm going shopping later,' Kira said. 'Maybe tomorrow.'

'Yes, maybe,' Gary said.

On one particular Tuesday, though, everything changed. Gary silently walked to school by himself. He did not want to play or talk to anyone. He worked silently in class, did not ask any questions and looked serious.

At playtime, Kira went up to him. 'You OK?' she asked.

(continued on next page)

Brilliant Stories for Assemblies
© Paul Urry

There was no reply. She looked around, 'Where's Paul?'

'In hospital. We had a phone call last night. Paul can have his operation today.'

Kira was stunned. She realized how important this was and how serious the operation could be. She put her arm around Gary.

All the anxiety, fear and emotion that Gary had kept hidden from his friends was suddenly released as Kira stayed near him and he began to cry. His classmates came over, not to laugh, but to help their friend.

Gary stayed quiet all day and went home with his Grandad. That night there was a phone call. Paul was doing well, the operation had been a success, but it would take a long time for Paul to get better.

Follow-up questions
◆ Could you have been as patient as Gary?
◆ Why did Gary need his friends to be there for him?

Brilliant Stories for Assemblies
© Paul Urry

This page may be photocopied by the purchasing institution only.

61

Friendship
(Helping with work)

'I want this work finished by the end of the lesson or you will have to miss playtime,' the teacher said to the class.

Lauren looked at her work – she was nowhere near finished. She was having problems spelling the words she needed. She looked around the table. Other children were nearly there. Paige caught her eye.

'You OK,' she asked.

'I can't do this. I need some help, but the teacher is working with another group.'

'Here, let me help. What's the problem?'

'I know what I want to say,' Lauren said, 'but I think the spellings are all wrong.'

Paige looked at Lauren's book. She was right. Most of the words were mis-spelt. She rubbed out some of the words and whispered the correct spellings to Lauren. Every time Lauren needed help, Paige would stop what she was doing and help out.

At playtime, Paige stayed behind even though she had finished her own work.

'Thanks Paige. I was really struggling there.'

'That's OK,' Paige smiled, 'I think that spelling is easy. I just know how to do it.'

The two girls went out to play smiling and chatting. They had always been in the same class, but Lauren always knew that Paige was better than her at her school work.

Later that week, Lauren sat in class thinking about how helpful and nice Paige was. She really wished that she was as good as her.

'What do you think, Lauren?' her teacher asked.

Lauren looked around. She had no idea what her teacher had said because she had been daydreaming.

'Uum, I'm not sure,' she hesitated.

'Not sure?' her teacher smiled. 'I thought you would like an extra games session.'

'Games? Yes please!' she said excitedly.

Everyone got changed and raced outside. The tennis nets had been put out already and the rackets and balls were on one side.

'Choose a partner and count how many times you can hit the ball to each other without stopping,' her teacher said. Lauren and Paige ran up to each other.

Lauren served, but Paige missed the ball completely. She tried again and again, but still Paige kept missing the ball.

'You try hitting it this time,' Lauren said.

Paige did, but every time she hit it, either it was too long or it hit the net. Lauren went up to her. 'I've been watching. You are holding the racket in the wrong way.' She showed her how to stand. 'Now stay on your toes and keep your eye on the ball.'

Paige managed to get the ball over the net. Lauren raced to it and got the ball back. Paige kept her eye on the ball and managed to hit it – straight into the net.

(continued on next page)

Brilliant Stories for Assemblies
© Paul Urry

'Don't worry,' Lauren called. 'Try again.'

Over the rest of the lesson Paige got better and better.

'Thanks, Lauren, I was really struggling there.'

'That's OK,' Lauren smiled. 'Tennis is easy. I just know how to do it.'

Follow-up questions

Paige and Lauren were both good at something.

◆ What are your special talents?
◆ Do you help others?

Brilliant Stories for Assemblies
© Paul Urry

This page may be photocopied by the purchasing institution only.

63

Friendship
(Starting a new school)

Lucy held her mum's hand tightly. They stood in the playground watching the other children. They had just moved to London from Birmingham because of her dad's new job.

As the whistle blew, she went to her class line. Standing there, she waved as her mum walked home. She looked at her new class and said nothing.

As they settled in the classroom, her teacher introduced her.

'This is Lucy. I am sure you will make her feel welcome. Would you tell us about yourself, please, Lucy?'

'Well …' she hesitated and looked at everyone, 'I am good at maths and … art. I like riding …' She stopped. Some people in the class were starting to giggle and laugh.

Her teacher looked up crossly. 'Laurelle, Faye, what's going on?'

The two girls looked at each other and started giggling again. Their teacher was now furious. 'How dare you be so rude to a new member of our school? Now tell me what the problem is.'

Faye looked up first. 'She speaks in a funny way.'

Her teacher was stunned. Lucy was embarrassed. In Birmingham everyone spoke with the same accent. Why were they being so rude?

Her new teacher let her take the register to the office. Whilst she was out he spoke to the class about what had happened.

When Lucy came back, she sat in her new place but did not look at anyone. They had all stopped laughing, but her classmates did not really talk to her.

At playtime, she stayed by the wall and watched. A couple of children asked her to play, but she politely and sadly refused. The rest of the day went the same way. Children tried to talk to her, but Lucy was so upset about what had happened before that she stayed by herself. Her teacher tried to get her to join in as well, but nothing worked. Lucy just wanted it to be home time so she could see her mum and dad.

She waited until she got home and then she started to cry.

'I want to go back to Birmingham,' she sobbed. 'I hate everyone here. They don't like me.' Her parents looked at each other sadly.

Just then, the doorbell rang.

'Is Lucy there?'

Lucy walked out into the hall and saw Faye. Faye could see that Lucy had been crying.

'I've come to apologize. I didn't mean to upset you. It's just that I've never heard anyone speak with an accent like yours. I got into a lot of trouble.'

Lucy's face relaxed.

'Would you like to come to the park? A lot of our class meet there in the evening. They want to see you.'

(continued on next page)

Brilliant Stories for Assemblies
© Paul Urry

Lucy's mum and dad smiled at each other then looked at Lucy.

'I don't know ...' she hesitated.

'Please? Come back if you don't want to stay.'

Lucy wiped her face and slowly walked out the door to the park.

Follow-up questions
◆ What do you think happened next?
◆ Would you be brave enough to apologize?

Vandalism
(Against children's work)

Vikki and Hayley looked at their work on the wall. They had spent ages writing it up and decorating it. They could see that the work was good. As they scanned the work of the rest of their class, they kept pausing to have a closer look at all the good things they could see.

Layton did not bother to look at the wall. He knew that his work was not there. He had not even bothered to finish his. He had to stay in at playtime, but even then he would not finish it. As everyone fussed over the work and looked for theirs, Layton just sat down and got angry with everyone, thinking that they were just showing off.

The next day, looking over to the display of work, Hayley noticed that something wasn't quite right. She stood up and went over to it. To her horror she saw that someone had got a felt-tip pen and drawn over some of the words.

'Miss!' she shouted. 'Look what's happened.' Miss Griffin went over and saw that not just Hayley's work but several pieces had been deliberately vandalized.

'Does anyone know who did this?' Miss Griffin asked.

The class looked around the room. Layton said nothing.

At lunchtime Hayley and Vikki kept asking people who had done it. But nobody had seen anything.

'Layton, did you see who ruined our work?'

'No,' he said abruptly, and walked away.

That afternoon they had art. Layton did not enjoy most subjects, but he loved art. They had to sketch some flowers in a plastic vase on their table. Layton carefully sketched the outline of the flower – each petal, leaf and detail. He then started to fill in all the shades and patterns he could see, looking up, drawing a little bit, and then looking up again at the flowers. Slowly and carefully, a beautiful picture was created. Layton was really pleased with it.

'That's fantastic,' Miss Griffin said. 'Look at the detail, shapes and shades. Well done, Layton!'

He held it up and showed everyone, a huge grin on his face. As Miss Griffin went around collecting the work, she leaned over to reach Layton's paper. Unfortunately, her sleeve caught the top of a flower and knocked over the vase. Some water spilled out of the vase and onto Layton's work.

'Sorry, Layton. Don't worry, it will dry.'

But Layton did worry and he did get cross.

'That's one of the best pieces of work I have ever done,' he shouted. The class stared at him. 'I can't believe it. My work is ruined!' He looked up. In front of him was the work on the wall. He stopped shouting as he understood how Vikki and Hayley had felt.

Follow-up questions
◆ What did Layton understand?
◆ Have you ever had a piece of work vandalized?

Brilliant Stories for Assemblies
© Paul Urry

Vandalism
(Against private property)

'An old witch lives in that house,' Sean said to Adam one day on their way back from school.

'Really?' Adam replied, looking through the broken fence into the back garden. 'It looks empty to me.'

The boys stared. The garden looked as though it had never been cut. Around the outside were some overgrown bushes with bees and butterflies around them. In the centre of the garden was a large apple tree.

'Fancy an apple?' Adam dared Sean.

'That's stealing,' Sean answered.

'And …?'

Looking around, Adam slipped through a hole in the fence into the garden. Sean quickly followed. They waded through the tall grass and started to climb the tree. The apples were ripe and juicy. The boys sat in the tree, eating the apples and throwing down the cores. Finally, when they were full up, they jumped down from the tree and went home.

The next day they went back to the garden through the fence and climbed the tree.

'Here, watch this,' Adam said. After finishing his apple he threw it at one of the back windows but hit the wall.

'That's rubbish! Here, watch this.' Sean threw his whole apple and hit the window. It bounced off.

'OK then,' Adam said, jumping down from the tree. He picked up a stone and threw it at the same window. It smashed immediately and glass fell to the ground.

'Quick, run!' Sean shouted, as a face appeared at the neighbour's window.

'Did you see how far I threw that?' Sean boasted. They went home laughing and joking. 'Shall we go back tomorrow?' Sean asked.

'Of course,' Adam replied. 'I can't let you beat me at something.'

Again, after school, they climbed through the fence and straight away started throwing stones at the windows, hiding amongst the tall bushes so that the neighbours could not see them.

This time Adam managed to break a window first.

'Right,' said Sean, picking up an even bigger stone. 'Watch thi …'

'Shhh,' whispered Adam, pointing behind him.

By the fence were two police officers peering through the gap. The boys hid in the tall grass, watching to see what would happen next.

After what seemed like ages the police officers walked away but, just as the boys began to relax, they came back. This time they came through the fence and started to walk around the garden. There was nowhere to hide. The police officers saw them and grabbed them before they could run off. They marched them out through the fence and into the back of their police car.

When Sean and Adam arrived at the police station their parents were asked to come and meet them there.

Follow-up questions
- What could happen to Adam and Sean?
- What would their parents say?
- Why do you think they broke the windows?

Vandalism
(Against personal property)

Glen had been looking forward to the weekend for ages. He and his dad were going to paint the fence at the front of their house. Glen loved painting – especially getting messy! The fence had needed doing for a long time – it was cracked and untidy.

Early next morning Glen had his breakfast put on his old clothes, went outside and suddenly stopped … it was freezing.

'Can we do this another day, Dad?' he asked. 'It's really cold.'

'You'll be OK,' his dad reassured him.

They took the lid off the tin and started to paint. Glen giggled as the paint splattered over his clothes and face. His dad laughed as well. As they painted, Glen's hands got colder and colder. It was starting to hurt to hold onto the paintbrush. His mum brought out some hot drinks and cake. Glen was having a great time, even if he was cold.

'You're doing a great job there,' said Chantelle, Glen's friend, as she went by. 'You must be freezing.' Glen nodded, but smiled.

By the middle of the afternoon, the fence was done. Glen stepped back with a huge grin of satisfaction on his face. He went in and took off his paint-covered clothes. Warming up, he jumped into the bath. Next day Chantelle and Adam came round to play. Glen pointed at his fence. They were very impressed.

On Wednesday something terrible happened. Adam was first to see it. He knocked at Glen's door on the way to school.

'Have you seen it?' he asked.

'What?'

'Your fence.'

The boys walked down the path and, to his horror, Glen saw that during the night someone had written all over the fence. On another part some names had been carved into the wood by something sharp. Glen's heart sank. His lovely painted fence – ruined.

'Why would anyone do that? They could see all the work we'd done.'

As they told Chantelle and other friends, they found out that some bigger children had been hanging around Glen's street the night before.

The rest of the week went quickly. Every time Glen walked past his fence, he looked and felt sad. On Saturday morning, though, there was a knock at the door. It was Chantelle and Adam both dressed in old clothes.

'We've spoken to your dad and we've come to help re-do the fence,' they said.

Glen got changed and ran outside. His dad was filling in the scratches and Adam and Chantelle were busy painting. Glen smiled.

'Thank you,' he said. 'Some people may not care about how they ruin things, but we cannot let them think they have upset us.' And with that he started painting.

Follow-up questions
◆ Why did the vandals ruin the fence?
◆ How do you think Adam felt when he saw the fence?

Brilliant Stories for Assemblies
© Paul Urry

The environment
(School)

In the corner of the playground was a small group of trees. In the summer, when it got hot, children would sit under them in the cool breeze. Heather liked to mess about by the trees. When the adults were not looking, she would often climb them and throw things at people.

'Leave it out, Hev,' shouted her best friend, Natalie.

One day Heather decided to throw small twigs at Natalie. 'There won't be anything left of the tree when you've finished!' Natalie teased.

Hidden from view among the leaves, Heather continued to break off twigs. Eventually she grew bored and climbed down. Looking around she saw all the leaves and twigs lying on the ground and laughed.

'Here watch this, Nat,' she called. Walking behind the tree she got a pair of school scissors from her pocket and started to dig into the bark and cut out letters.

'Don't write your own name, Hev. That'll be stupid. Everyone will know it's you!' Natalie pointed out.

'Oh yeah,' said Heather, and she began to change it into a pattern as the sap began to ooze from the bark. 'Here, you have a go, Nat,' she said, passing her the scissors.

After Natalie had carved her pattern into the bark they got bored and walked away. For a couple of days after that they continued to cut patterns into the trees. Several weeks later, the children started to notice that the trees were changing. It was the middle of summer, but the leaves were falling off the trees and the branches were starting to sag. Everyone was called into assembly.

'Some of you may have noticed that the trees are dying,' the head said to a stunned school. 'Some children have cut into the bark and now the trees have got a disease and will have to be cut down.'

The children left the hall in silence. The next day they watched as a man and a woman, wearing special protective clothes, came and cut down the trees.

'The playground looks empty without the trees,' a quiet Natalie said to the teacher. 'Could we plant more trees?'

'That would be a good idea.'

'We could ask for people to give money and plants to make the playground even better than it was before,' Natalie continued.

Her teacher was surprised – Natalie did not usually offer suggestions – but she agreed to it. The idea caught the imagination of the whole school. People sent in money, sold biscuits and donated plants.

On a sunny Saturday morning, children, parents and teachers turned up to plant the new playground. The first people to arrive were … Natalie and Heather.

Follow-up questions
◆ Why did they vandalize the trees?
◆ Why didn't they tell anyone they had done it?

Brilliant Stories for Assemblies
© Paul Urry

This page may be photocopied by the purchasing institution only.

69

The environment
(Growing food)

'I've got a surprise for you, Sarah,' her dad said one spring day.

'Is it a doll? Or some sweets? Or a book?' she asked.

'Not quite,' her dad hesitated, and gave her a small bag.

Sarah looked in. At the bottom were two small green plants. She was very disappointed. 'Is that all? Two plants?'

'Get them out,' her dad said, 'They're a bit special, have a look at the labels.'

Sarah picked one out complaining that she'd got some soil on her hands, and read the label. It said 'Tomato plant'. She picked the second one out. 'Strawberry,' she said lazily.

'Well what do you think?' her dad asked eagerly.

'What do I think about what?' she asked puzzled.

'You like tomatoes and strawberries. I thought you could grow your own.'

Sarah just stared blankly at him. She could see the enthusiasm in his eyes so decided not to disappoint him. 'What do we do?' she asked, trying to sound interested.

'We need to find two large pots and fill them with some compost. Then we need to plant them right away.'

'Will I get dirty?' she asked.

Her dad ignored that comment and they went into the garden together. They found two large pots, carefully put the compost in and, gently taking the plants out of their small containers, put them in the pots too.

'Now what?' she asked.

'Water them, of course.'

Sarah went into the house and filled up a watering can. She brought it out into the garden and poured it lazily over the plants.

'Careful!' her dad said. 'They are only small plants.'

For the next couple of weeks, her dad kept on reminding Sarah to water the plants. She always complained but did it in the end.

During the summer holidays Sarah watched as the plants grew. Flowers appeared and were replaced by fruit that gradually became ripe. She did not need to be told to water them now. She loved going outside and checking how they were doing.

'Dad,' she called one day, 'Look, this strawberry is ready to eat!'

Her dad bent down. It was a beautiful deep red colour and looked delicious.

'Pick it then,' he said.

Carefully she took the fruit from the plant and ran in to show her mum.

'Aren't you going to eat it?' her dad said. 'There are going to be lots more!'

(continued on next page)

Brilliant Stories for Assemblies
© Paul Urry

After she had washed it and taken the stem off she took a bite. It tasted so rich, so juicy. It was better than any other strawberry she had ever had.

'Thanks, Dad, the plants were a great surprise.'

Follow-up questions
- Have you ever grown any food?
- Do you think it is easy growing food?

Brilliant Stories for Assemblies
© Paul Urry

This page may be photocopied by the purchasing institution only.

71

Bullying

It did not happen all the time, but Ben was always careful not to upset Tom. They had not been friends since Year Three when Ben started at the school. Tom had always hurt Ben. Sometimes Tom kicked, hit or pinched him. Nobody ever saw it happen. It was always in school. On some days it was in lessons and on other days it was at playtimes but Tom always hurt him, and it always upset him. It was worse for Ben that it did not happen every day; sometimes weeks would go by and nothing would happen.

Ben and Tom were now in Year Six. A visitor had come to school to talk about their new high school. The woman was joking about some of the stories they might hear – older children flushing bags down the toilet or new children being dared to do silly or dangerous things and, finally, bullying. Ben looked over to where Tom was sitting. Tom was smiling and quietly looked back over to Ben.

Ben's heart began to race. He felt tears well up in his eyes. The teacher said that these things did not happen because the school listened to any worries the pupils had. Ben was scared because he knew he couldn't say anything.

Ben did not go to school the next day. He told his mum that he was not well. Instead, he lay in bed, not talking to anyone, whilst he thought how much worse the bullying would get at secondary school.

After three days of pretending he was ill his mum told him he was to go to school. Ben nervously walked into the playground but did not play football as usual. He just watched Tom. He sat on the wall. Nothing happened, he was just thinking.

In class Ben could not concentrate on his work. Tom did nothing until lunchtime when, on the way out to lunch, he hit Ben hard in his back. It made him fall to the ground.

Ben looked round. No one saw it. He started to cry. He thought about Tom, the secondary school and how disappointed his parents would be in him. All these thoughts filled his head at the same time. He sat on the floor, put his head in his folded arms and quietly wept.

Soon after, he felt a gentle hand on his shoulder. Ben slowly looked up and saw his teacher. She said nothing but helped him up and took him somewhere quiet. Ben told the teacher everything. His teacher said she would have to tell others. Ben sadly nodded.

That afternoon Ben helped in the infants. He saw Tom going to the headteacher's room. He saw him come out upset and trying not to cry and at the end of the day he saw Tom's parents come into school. For the first time since Year Two his mum was also waiting for him after school. She gave him a big hug and held him tightly as they walked home.

Follow-up question
◆ How could Ben have stopped Tom earlier?

Brilliant Stories for Assemblies
© Paul Urry

Perseverance

'But it's hard, Dad,' Eleanor complained as she tried to swim without floats.

'I know, but you need to use the floats first,' her dad replied

'But I want to swim now!' demanded Eleanor.

Her dad laughed. 'I know, but you need to take your time. If you want to learn something new you need to practise and gradually get better.'

Eleanor frowned. 'That'll take AGES and I want to do it now!'

Her dad lifted her up out of the pool. 'Let's have some fun,' he said. 'Jump in and I will catch you.'

'But it will splash and I'll get my hair wet!'

'You have to get wet – it's a swimming pool,' her dad chuckled.

Eleanor looked at the pool. She saw her dad smiling and holding his arms out. With a big shout she closed her eyes and jumped. Into the air she went and splashed into the water. Her dad caught her before she went under. After he had got the water out of his eye, he saw a huge smile on Eleanor's face.

'Again!' she cheered.

Every time she did it, she jumped higher and landed further in the water. They carried on playing in the water with the floats.

'Time to go now,' her dad said.

The week went quickly. Next time they went to the pool Eleanor jumped in and swam with the floats. She even tried to put her head under the water!

As the weeks went by, Eleanor got more confident in the water. She could swim a whole length with floats. She also began to swim on her back, looking high up to the roof of the swimming pool. Above all, though, she loved splashing her dad with her hands and the floats.

One day in the pool, Eleanor's dad took her floats away. Eleanor felt funny. There was nothing keeping her head above the water and she quickly slipped under it. She tried kicking her legs and moving her arms but she still could not get her head above the water. Her dad picked her up and put her down in the water again.

'This time, kick your legs more,' he said. Eleanor tried. It was hard. But with her dad holding her hands, she was able to swim.

'I'm doing it! I'm doing it!' she spluttered and then sank under the water again.

'You're getting there,' her dad said.

The next week she swam a bit further with no floats, then even further. She tried so hard one time that *she* asked to stop.

'I'm tired today,' she said.

'I'm not surprised. You have tried really hard today. Let's stop now and come back next week.'

'But I want to carry on!' Eleanor pleaded.

(continued on next page)

'Next week,' her dad reassured her.

Eventually Eleanor was able to swim on her front and her back. She remembered the time when she could not swim and all the fun she had had learning.

Follow-up question
◆ Can you think of something you once couldn't do, but now you can because you persevered?

Brilliant Stories for Assemblies
© Paul Urry

Jealousy

Samantha was a great runner. She could run for hours. She never knew why she was so good, but she loved running, especially as she found some schoolwork difficult. Clare, however, was good at schoolwork. She was jealous of Sam because she was so popular.

Clare thought of how she could become more popular than Sam. Eventually it came to her – to beat her in a race! But she was not a good athlete, so she started to train every day and every day she got faster and could run further.

Sam looked forward to the summer and in particular to Sports Day. The whole school would go down to the park and have a great time. The last race was the long distance, where you had to run around the whole park. Only a few people took part, but the same person won every year – Sam.

A week before Sports Day the teacher asked who wanted to enter each race. 'Can we do the sack race?' said some of the children. Others chose the obstacle, sprint, egg and spoon, and relay races. Sam just waited. Finally the teacher asked for the distance race. Sam put her hand up and, to her surprise, so did Clare.

'You can't run that far,' Clare's friends said. But of course she could.

Sports Day arrived. It was a bright, warm day. Lots of parents were there and all the children were cheering.

'And finally,' said the headteacher, 'could I have the competitors for the distance race. 'I'm going to beat you,' Clare said to Sam nastily as they lined up together. Sam was shocked.

'Go!' The race started, the cheering grew louder and Clare ran into the lead. Sam started to chase after her. Both girls were clear of the rest of the children. Slowly she caught up with Clare, who couldn't believe it when Sam ran past her. Clare was now even more determined and caught up with Sam. The cheering crowd had faded into the distance as they went round the first corner of the park. Now Sam was almost sprinting, Clare stayed with her. She couldn't believe it. Was she going to be beaten?

Matching each other step for step they weren't watching where they were running. As they turned the second corner, Clare did not notice a tree root poking out of the ground. She tripped over with such a force she went flying through the air, and landed heavily on the ground. Sam looked over her shoulder as she ran away from her. Clare was not getting up. Sam stopped running and went back to see her.

'Are you OK?' she asked.

'What do you care?' snapped Clare.

Together they looked at Clare's ankle. It had swelled up. Sam waved to the teachers on the other side of the park. While they waited for help to come, the other runners caught up and ran past them.

'Carry on and win the race,' Clare said to Sam.

'No. I'll wait till a teacher gets here.'

'Go on! I'll be OK.'

(continued on next page)

Sam looked up; the teachers were nearly there. 'Look after yourself,' she said to Clare.

'Win the race,' Clare smiled.

Sam stood up and started to jog, the jog turned into a run and the run soon turned into a sprint. The leaders were turning the final corner of the race. She was now flying. The crowd had seen what she had done and, as she got nearer to the last turn, she could hear them cheering her on. She passed some children who were so tired they had slowed to a walk. Tenth, nineth, eighth, she was passing children as if they weren't there. With only a couple of hundred metres to go she was now third. Her face was screwed up in agony. She had never run so fast or hard in her life. Into the last hundred metres. She went into second. With every step she was getting closer and closer to the leader. The noise from the crowd was deafening. Into the last ten metres and she had nearly caught the leader. With a lunge she dived for the line, fell over and lay on the ground exhausted.

A teacher walked over, picked her up and gave her a card … second place. The winner jumped up and down and was mobbed by her friends.

Sam went home that night tired and fed up. That evening she stayed in her room. She had never lost a race before. Next day she walked to school by herself.

In assembly the prizes were given out for the winners. Sam sat there trying to smile and clap although she was so disappointed.

'And finally,' said the headteacher, 'a special award. We have someone here who would like to present it.' From a side door came Clare on crutches. Her ankle was bandaged up, but she was smiling.

'For exceptional sportsmanship, the award goes to … Sam.' The whole school cheered and clapped so loudly Sam was embarrassed.

Clare gave her the prize and said, 'I'm sorry for being so jealous of you. You are a great person and a fantastic runner. Can I be your friend please?'

Sam smiled and nodded. She faced her school again and saw everyone clapping.

Follow-up questions
◆ Was Sam right to go back for Clare?
◆ Can you think of someone you are jealous of?

Brilliant Stories for Assemblies
© Paul Urry

Jumping to conclusions

It all began yesterday. I was away for a week with my classmates in Year Six on an adventure holiday. Two of the class were walking through the woods when suddenly, for no apparent reason, they stopped, looked over their shoulders and heard a sound – something was moving. In the darkness through the trees they could see two green, narrow eyes staring at them in the distance. They looked again and – just as quickly – the eyes were gone. The boys glanced at each other and ran quickly back to their room. They told all of us about what had happened. No one went near the woods again that day.

That evening we had to walk back through the woods again on our way from the river. Silently, we stayed close to each other, looking around.

'Arghhh,' some children at the front screamed. We rushed up to them. A girl was pointing into a gap between two trees in the distance. Something was moving, but we couldn't see it. Our teacher told us to calm down. We all sprinted back to our rooms and gathered round the children who had screamed. Eventually, they told us of the fiery green staring eyes that suddenly appeared in front of them.

'Rubbish!' shouted Amy. 'There's nothing there, you're just panicking.' We all looked at her, unsure what to say. 'Right! I'll prove it.' She stood up and asked if anyone was going to come with her. Nobody moved. She confidently walked towards the wood. Then she started to run. We watched as she disappeared into the distance. We waited.

Silence.

Suddenly there was a distant shout 'Nooooo!' then nothing. It was Amy's voice.

We ran to the teachers and told them what had happened. It was getting darker now but we all walked nervously into the wood, staying very close to each other. We all called Amy's name out, but she didn't call back. We went deeper into the wood, all the time looking over our shoulders. Suddenly, there was a shout from a teacher. They had found her! She had tripped over a root whilst running and hurt her leg. We all relaxed as we could see that she was OK. The teachers picked her up and started to carry her out. We began to joke and smile.

'Shhh,' said a teacher nervously. We froze. There was a sound behind us. I looked over my shoulder. It was too dark to see properly. There were sounds in front, behind and to the sides of us. We could hear things in the silence of the wood, then they stopped. As my eyes got used to the darkness I could see a pair of eyes. Then another. I was too scared to move. They were getting closer to my teacher; there was panic on his face … then he relaxed and smiled. We wondered what was going on. Then I saw. Standing in the clearing with bright green eyes was … a family of rabbits!

Follow-up questions
◆ How could the children have stopped themselves getting frightened?
◆ What would you have done?

Bravery

It was Friday. Everyone loved Friday. It was games. Their teacher would often say that she had never seen a class get changed for games as quickly as this one.

Once out on the field, the teams set up the rounders field. They warmed up and were ready to play. The game went well. Both teams were really good.

During the second innings, Adam hit the ball as hard as he could. It went soaring into the air right to the back of the field. James and Sophie both ran for the catch, James from the right and Sophie from the left. Everyone watched as, slowly, the ball began to come down. Both children had their eyes fixed on the ball. At the last moment their teacher, and everyone else, saw what was going to happen. It was too late to shout out.

THUD!

The two children ran into each other at full speed, both fell heavily to the ground. James got up. Sophie did not.

Everyone ran over to see if they were OK. As their teacher arrived he saw Sophie sit up and hold her arm.

'It hurts so much,' she sobbed.

Her teacher asked her where it hurt and if she could move her fingers. Realizing that it was serious he asked the class to line up. Without a fuss they did.

Another teacher took the class back to their room whilst Sophie was taken to the office. All the time she held onto her arm, bravely answering questions despite the incredible pain. At the office, her teacher phoned for an ambulance and called her mum.

'Sophie, are you OK?' her mum asked when she arrived.

Holding back the tears, Sophie joked, 'Don't panic, Mum. I'm all right.'

'Of course you're not,' her mum said.

Sophie started laughing but stopped as it made her arm hurt even more.

The ambulance arrived quickly. The paramedics did lots of tests and asked questions. All the time Sophie kept calm and answered them politely.

'You can cry, shout out or hit something,' the paramedics laughed. But Sophie kept calm. Still crying a little she smiled at her mum as they got into the ambulance.

The teacher went back to class, where everyone looked worried.

'You have a very special classmate,' she said. 'As they were leaving, the paramedics said to me that they rarely meet such a brave and strong person. Although she has hurt herself and has gone to hospital she is thinking about you. She told me to let you know she is OK and she will ring some of you tonight.'

Quietly in the corner sat James. The teacher looked over to him. 'She told me to tell you that it was an accident and that she doesn't blame you at all.' James smiled and rubbed his bruised shoulder.

Follow-up questions
◆ Would you have reacted like Sophie?
◆ How could you have kept as calm as she did?

Brilliant Stories for Assemblies
© Paul Urry

Making the right decisions

Note: In this story there are places to pause and reflect on the right decisions although there is only one sequence.

Daniel and Joseph were having a great time on holiday with their Gran. It was a beautiful day, they were on their bikes and, of course, there was no school!

'Come on, Joseph,' Daniel ordered, 'let's ride to the old castle.'

'I don't know,' Joseph said, 'It could be dangerous.'

'I'm your big brother. I'll look after you,' Daniel said, riding off down the path.

Joseph hesitated, but started to follow when he realized that Daniel was not going to stop.

When they arrived at the broken gates, there was no one around.

'Come on, let's explore.'

'I'll wait here,' Joseph said.

'Chicken!' Daniel shouted as he rode up to the front door.

(What should Joseph do? Go with Daniel, stay or go back to their Gran's house. Why?)

'Wait for me!' he shouted.

Daniel pushed the front door. It was locked. Then he went up to one of the windows and threw stones at it until it broke. Carefully clearing the glass away he made a hole big enough to climb through.

(What should Joseph do? Why?)

Joseph looked around. There was no one about and he felt scared. He followed his brother into the dusty and dark room.

'Look at all these things,' Daniel said, blowing dust and cobwebs off different broken objects. 'Let's go upstairs.'

Joseph looked around. It was darker in the castle and a lot colder than outside. As he followed his brother he heard a shout.

'Noooooo!'

He ran around the corner and saw his brother lying at the foot of the stairs. There was blood coming out of his mouth and head. Joseph ran over.

'Daniel! Daniel!' he shouted, 'Can you hear me?'

Daniel lay on the ground not moving. Joseph watched as Daniel eventually moved a finger.

(What should Joseph do? Stay with his brother? Get help? Try to carry him out?)

'Stay here, Daniel. I will go and get help. I promise I'll be back. Don't try to move.' He ran out of the room, back through the window and rode off to the nearest house. Banging on the door he told the young man what had happened. The man rang for an ambulance and Daniel telephoned his Gran. He quickly rode back to the castle gates.

(Should Joseph go in and see Daniel or wait for the ambulance? Why?)

(continued on next page)

'The ambulance is on its way!' Joseph shouted. Daniel did not reply.

As the ambulance drew up Joseph showed them where to go. The paramedics treated him and carried him off to hospital where his Gran was waiting.

Follow-up question
◆ Did Joseph do the right thing?

Brilliant Stories for Assemblies
© Paul Urry

The Sphinx
(Ancient Greece)

Props suggested
Picture of the Egyptian Sphinx. A walking stick.

About two and a half THOUSAND years ago, great stories were told throughout the Greek world about monsters and beasts who helped or hurt people. Some of these monsters lived in the sea, others in the sky and some on the land.

One of these monsters was the Sphinx. It had the head of a goddess and the body of a lion – with its strong claws. Now this Sphinx used to sit by the side of a popular road. As travellers came past it would jump out and give them a riddle:

What has four legs in the morning, two legs at midday and three legs in the evening?

If they failed to answer it, she would eat them! Unfortunately nobody was able to answer the riddle. People who lived in the area, were so scared of the Sphinx that nobody went down that road. Instead, they took the longer route around.

One day, however, a traveller called Oedipus was visiting that part of Greece. He had not heard the story of the Sphinx and walked down the road on his way to the town. Suddenly the Sphinx jumped out in front of him.

'In order to pass you must answer a riddle. If you cannot you will die.'

Oedipus looked round; there was no one to save him. He could not run away as the Sphinx was much stronger and quicker than he was. So he said, 'I will try. What is the riddle?'

'What has four legs in the morning, two legs at midday and three legs in the evening?'

Oedipus thought for a while. This was a really hard riddle. How could something have a different number of legs? He was beginning to worry when it suddenly occurred to him.

'The answer is … man,' he said confidently.

The Sphinx was taken aback. *How did he get it right? Perhaps he has just guessed*, she thought. *I will test him again.*

'Why is it man?' she asked.

'In the morning of a man's life he has four legs, he crawls on his hands and knees. In the midday of his life he has two legs, he walks on his feet. And in the evening of his life he has three legs – the two he walks on and a walking stick.'

The Sphinx was furious that someone had solved her riddle and she ran off leaving the town far behind.

When the townspeople found out what had happened, they were overjoyed and allowed Oedipus to marry their queen.

Follow-up question
◆ Did you think of the answer before Oedipus?

Brilliant Stories for Assemblies
© Paul Urry

This page may be photocopied by the purchasing institution only.

81

The wooden horse of Troy
(Ancient Greece)

Props suggested

Copy of *The Iliad* by Homer.

It is thought that this could be one of the very first stories ever written down. It is thousands of years old. No one knows who wrote the story but people think it was an Ancient Greek called Homer. It is a story about a war between the Greeks and the Trojans.

The story starts when the prince of the Trojans, Paris, steals Helen, the wife of an important Greek prince. The Greek prince is so furious that he gathers an army and they sail to the city of Troy.

Unfortunately Troy had a huge wall around it and the Greeks could not get into the city. There were lots of battles, some of which the Greeks won, others that the Trojans won. This went on for TEN years.

After all those years, the Greeks realized that if they were going to get Helen back, they would have to have a clever plan.

The leader of the Greeks walked up to the walls of Troy and announced that they were going back to Greece, but before they did they wanted to leave a present.

The Trojans watched from their high walls as a huge wooden horse was wheeled up to the massive gates of Troy. Then they saw all the Greek soldiers go to their boats and sail away. They were extremely puzzled by what was happening and, at first, they thought it was a trick.

The Greeks left the wooden horse, as tall as a house, outside the gate all night. Meanwhile, some of the Greeks' greatest soldiers, who had been hiding, came out and climbed inside the horse and waited silently.

The next day the Trojans saw that the Greeks had definitely gone and started to celebrate. They wondered what to do with the horse and eventually opened their gates and hauled the horse into their city. They shook the horse, but the people inside kept quiet. They looked all over the horse for doors but could not see any. So finally they left it and continued to celebrate all day and, at night, they fell fast asleep.

When the soldiers were sure nobody was awake, they opened a secret door in the horse and crept out, drew their swords and attacked the Trojans. They got Helen back and won the war.

The gods were so furious that the Greeks had tricked the Trojans that they made sure the leaders had a terrible journey back to Greece. They made sure that the leader of the Greeks in the wooden horse, Odysseus, did not reach home for another ten years!

Follow-up question
◆ Why did the Trojans trust the Greeks?

Brilliant Stories for Assemblies
© Paul Urry

Boudicca
(Ancient Romans)

Props suggested
- Map of the South-east of England to show where Boudicca travelled and attacked.
- Picture of the statue of Boudicca opposite the Houses of Parliament.

When the Romans invaded England, they did not try to have lots of battles. Instead they made agreements with local leaders. If these leaders agreed not to attack the Romans, then the Romans would build them roads and baths and great theatres. Most of the people were happy with this, but some did not want the Romans in England at all.

One of the tribes that agreed to work with the Romans was the Iceni. They lived in East Anglia, around Norfolk. The king of the Iceni was happy to share what he had so that his people could live in peace and there would be no war. However, when the king died, the Romans wanted all of the land. His queen, Boudicca objected to this and the Romans had her and her daughters attacked and hurt.

This made Boudicca want revenge. She spoke to other local tribes and told them that, if this was how the Romans treated one tribe, they would do it to all of the others soon. Lots of tribes agreed to work with Boudicca.

Rather than wait for the Romans to attack them, the tribes attacked the capital of Roman England – Colchester. As they ran through the streets they burned houses and killed any Romans they found. They destroyed statues and public buildings. They were so terrifying that some Roman soldiers refused to attack Boudicca and her army. After the attack Colchester was completely destroyed. The Romans had never expected such an attack.

Boudicca was pleased with this, but she wanted more. Next she took her army to London. Here again, they destroyed the Roman parts of the town, burning houses, killing Romans and terrifying everyone who saw her.

Boudicca knew that the Romans would soon attack her, so she continued moving north from London. She came to St. Albans and for a third and final time, she destroyed the Roman town.

The Romans knew that she was not going to stop. They also knew she had a huge army. More Roman soldiers came from the north of the country and waited. Boudicca's army saw the Romans ahead and waited.

In a big clearing stood ten thousand Roman soldiers, facing one hundred thousand of Boudicca's army. Boudicca attacked. The Romans stayed still and waited for them to arrive. A huge battle started and the Romans began to win. Knowing they were losing, the tribes tried to escape but were blocked by all of their families, who had come to watch the battle. The Romans showed no mercy and killed everyone.

When Boudicca could see she had lost, she took poison rather than be captured. Today outside the Houses of Parliament in London there is a large statue of Boudicca riding her chariot and horses.

(continued on next page)

Follow-up questions

◆ Do you think Boudicca was a great leader?
◆ Do you think she was right to do what she did?

Brilliant Stories for Assemblies
© Paul Urry

Julius Caesar
(Ancient Romans)

Props suggested
Picture of Julius Caesar. A copy of the play by Shakespeare.

A hundred years before Jesus Christ was born, one of the most famous Romans, Julius Caesar, was born. Many things happened in his life; he was very ambitious, he loved being popular and enjoyed great battles. He changed the way Rome was led. Before Julius Caesar, people voted on the leaders they wanted, but after he died, there was only going to be one leader, an emperor, whom people did not vote for. There is not a happy ending in this story!

When Julius was younger he proved to be a brave soldier in the army, getting an award for saving the life of a friend in a battle when he could have been killed. When he was twenty-five he was captured by pirates and his family had to pay them to release him. He was so furious that he made sure the pirates were captured and, in front of everyone, he had them executed.

Julius wanted to be even more powerful. As he grew older he got elected to the government, called the Senate. There he paid people money to support him. Roman people loved Julius because he was such a great general. Wherever he took his army he won great battles.

Fifty years before Jesus was born, Julius even brought an army over to England but only stayed for a couple of months. Whilst he was away from Rome he made sure that his friends were in charge and did what he wanted.

He joined forces with two other great leaders – Crassus and Pompey. Crassus had lots of money and supported the battles of the other two. Pompey was also a great general. However, Crassus died and Julius and Pompey both wanted to be the only leader. Pompey persuaded some of the leaders of Rome that Julius wanted to become a king and when he came back from another great victory they told him not to come into Rome.

Julius was furious with this but still went into the great city. This started a war between those who wanted Julius and those who wanted Pompey. Pompey was killed and Julius returned to Rome to a cheering crowd. He gave important jobs to his friends and everyone was frightened of his great power. But the people of Rome still liked him.

On 15th March, forty-four years before Jesus was born, and only one month after Julius Caesar had become leader of Rome, the sixty members of the government, the Senate, decided to get rid of him. They went into the hall with small daggers hidden underneath their clothes. One at a time they went up to Caesar and stabbed him until he was dead.

Julius Caesar is still an important figure today, as in our calendar one month is named after him.

Follow-up questions
◆ Which month is named after Julius Caesar?
◆ Why do you think Caesar wanted so much power?

Brilliant Stories for Assemblies
© Paul Urry

This page may be photocopied by the purchasing institution only.

85

The Gunpowder Plot
(Tudor times)

I walked down the steps into the darkness with the other guards. All we were told was that we were looking for someone or something. This was the second time we had been sent down to the cellars underneath the Houses of Parliament. It felt cold in the autumn darkness. We held our lamps out in front of us and nervously walked down the steps. Once we were at the bottom we carefully crept around.

Silence.

I pointed to different guards and showed them where I wanted them to look. They looked scared, but did it. Out of the corner of my eye I thought I spotted some movement. It was too big to be a rat, so I walked over, holding my lamp high. As my eyes got used to the darkness I saw a pair of eyes, then the whole person. I stepped back but he didn't run or shout. Instead he just stood up and allowed other guards to tie his hands together. As I looked around where he had been I counted thirty-six barrels of gunpowder. With such a huge amount of explosives he would have blown the Houses of Parliament to pieces – and everyone inside it, including King James!

We marched the man back up the stairs and into the November night and off to the king. The king was woken up but the man refused to say who he was and who was helping him. The king ordered that he be taken away and tortured until he told the truth.

As we took him away, we found out from some spies that his name was Guy Fawkes. We also found out where his friends had been hiding. Some had been killed in a battle and others had been captured.

I watched as he was tortured for two days. Eventually, he was placed on the rack. His wrists and ankles were tied and the torturer turned the handles. Guy called out in agony as slowly his body was stretched and his joints pulled apart. He confessed that he was trying to kill the king, but it took another six days of torture before he told the names of the others involved.

Guy Fawkes stood next to me during his short trial two months later. He was found guilty and four days later, it was my job to lead him through the streets to his execution. People along the way were shouting at him and throwing rotten food. I led him up the steps to the noose. He said nothing but let the executioner put the rope around his neck. After he had been killed his head was cut off and put on a spike for everyone to see the face of a traitor.

Follow-up questions
- How would you have felt seeing what the guard saw in the story?
- Would you have felt scared, nervous or nothing?
- What would you have asked Guy Fawkes if you had had the chance?
- What do you think he would have said?

This page may be photocopied by the purchasing institution only.

86

Brilliant Stories for Assemblies
© Paul Urry

The Spanish Armada
(Tudor times)

Props suggested
Map to show where Spain and England are. The route of the Armada. A picture of a Spanish galleon. Pictures of Philip II of Spain and Elizabeth I.

King Philip II of Spain was furious with England. Queen Elizabeth's father, Henry VIII, had argued with the Pope and although they were both Christians Henry VIII had created his own church. When Elizabeth became queen she continued to tell people to follow her father's church – the Church of England. Philip demanded that England become a Catholic country again. Elizabeth refused.

On the morning of 19th July 1588 Philip sent 130 boats – called an Armada – to attack England. Elizabeth expected this and went down to the docks where the soldiers and sailors stood. There she gave a great speech that made everyone cheer before going into battle. This was a fantastic achievement for a woman in Tudor times.

The Armada sailed up the English Channel and stayed at Calais in France. On 7th August, the English had a clever plan. At midnight, they filled eight ships with gunpowder and cannons. They lit the ships and sent them towards the Spanish fleet. The Spanish sailors woke up to hear a lot of explosions and noise. Looking around they saw these great ships attacking them – with no one on them!

Desperate to escape, they cut off their anchors and tried to get away, but there were so many ships that they collided with each other.

As the morning came the English ships attacked the Spanish Armada, sinking ships one by one.

But then, just as the English were expecting to win, the wind changed direction and the Spanish fleet managed to escape to the North Sea. The English chased after them. By the time the Armada and the English fleet had got to Newcastle, the English ships had run out of cannon balls and returned home.

The Spanish, meanwhile, had to sail all the way around the north of Scotland and the west of Ireland. They were hit by many storms and lost even more boats on the rocks. Starving, the Spanish finally managed to get back to Spain. They had lost nearly half of their ships and only 6,000 out of 26,000 men survived.

In England there were huge celebrations and the Spanish galleons never came back.

Follow-up questions
◆ Although Elizabeth did not fight, people thought she was a great queen. Why?
◆ How do you think the English soldiers and sailors felt when they were fighting?
◆ How do you think the Spanish soldiers and sailors felt when they were fighting?

Brilliant Stories for Assemblies
© Paul Urry

This page may be photocopied by the purchasing institution only.

87

Mary Seacole
(Victorian Britain)

Florence Nightingale was a brave woman who lived a hundred and fifty years ago. She was one of the first nurses to leave England and help soldiers wounded and dying in the Crimean war, thousand of miles away. She was celebrated in all the newspapers as the 'Lady with the Lamp' who, with her other nurses, helped many soldiers.

However, there was another famous nurse who helped soldiers. Her name was Mary Seacole. Mary was born in Jamaica in 1805. When she was 49 she came to England and asked if she could be a nurse in the army. She was told no for two reasons – firstly, because she had had no training as a nurse in England, and secondly, because she was black!

Mary was a determined person and decided to make her own way to the battlefield. Unlike Florence Nightingale, whose hospital was many miles away from the fighting, Mary opened a small nursing hotel close to the action. She frequently went out onto the battlefield to treat soldiers as they were injured, holding on to some who died in her arms. She was extremely brave and cared for others. The soldiers liked Mary because she was so kind and courageous. They called her 'Mother Seacole'.

Mary cooked food for some soldiers and developed her own medicine for treating illnesses. At the end of the war she returned to England with no money. Whilst all the newspapers were celebrating the great work of Florence Nightingale, Mary tried to find a way to get some money.

When the soldiers found out that Mary was so poor they were worried about her. They made sure that the papers celebrated her work as a black woman and also raised money to help her. Mary was so pleased she wrote a story about herself called the 'Wonderful Adventures of Mrs Seacole in Many Lands'. This became a bestseller and Mary was awarded lots of medals for her bravery.

Mary was a determined person who would not let people stop her doing things because of the colour of her skin. Every year on 14th May, the date of her death, people lay a wreath on her grave in London to show how important she was and that she has not been forgotten.

Follow-up questions
Mary Seacole could have been killed on the battlefield.

- ◆ Why do you think she went there?
- ◆ Why did others help her when she returned to England?

This page may be photocopied by the purchasing institution only.

88

Brilliant Stories for Assemblies
© Paul Urry

Charles Dickens
(Victorian Britain)

:Props suggested
• Picture of Charles Dickens and copies of
• his books.

Charles Dickens is most famous for writing *A Christmas Carol* in which Ebenezer Scrooge is visited by different ghosts. The ghosts turn him from a mean and miserable person to a happy and generous one. But Charles Dickens wrote much more than this story.

He was born in Portsmouth in February 1812 and moved to Kent when he was five. He loved to read books to find out about the world around him. However, when he was only twelve, his father got into debt and was sent to prison. Charles had to give up school and go to work in a factory. Even after his father was released from prison he carried on working at the factory for nearly a year.

When he returned to school he showed how clever and hard working he was. He quickly became an office boy for a firm of solicitors, an important job for a young man then.

Despite the good job, Charles was bored. He taught himself to write shorthand – a special way of writing that means you can quickly write down every word a person says without writing the whole word each time.

By the time he was only twenty he was working at the House of Commons, writing down what the Members of Parliament said using shorthand. He then became a successful journalist – someone who writes for newspapers – and then he started to write books.

His first book sold thousands! He quickly became quite rich and popular. He got married and eventually had ten children!

Despite his great success he remembered his own childhood. He saw that most people in London did not have clean water and worked long hours in factories for very little money. He wrote about the lives of people like this and made the government change laws to make everyone's life better.

He enjoyed writing his novels and short stories, but he also used to read some of the stories to huge crowds, because he knew that a lot of people could not read or write at that time and he wanted everyone to enjoy his stories.

Wherever he went thousands turned up. However he worked too hard, became ill and had to go and live in the countryside. His health got worse and he died in 1870 aged 58.

People were so upset and he was so important that he was buried in Westminster Abbey in London next to other famous poets and writers. There, today, you can see his name.

Follow-up questions
◆ Why was Charles Dickens so popular?
◆ Why do you think he worked so hard?

Brilliant Stories for Assemblies
© Paul Urry

This page may be photocopied by the purchasing institution only.

89

Sadako (Japan)
(20th century)

Props suggested
Books about Sadako and pictures of her and the monument to her. Instructions for making an origami paper crane from the Internet (there are many available).

In 1945, at the end of the Second World War, a nuclear bomb was dropped on the Japanese city of Hiroshima. Thousands of people died. Sadako Sasaki and her family were some of the lucky ones; they survived. Sadako was only two years old at the time. As she grew, Sadako became a great athlete, but when she was twelve years old she suddenly started to feel sick. She did not tell people for a long time, until one day she collapsed. She was rushed to hospital where they found she had leukaemia. The doctors explained that this was due to the radiation from the bomb ten years before. They also told her that she was going to get very ill and would probably die.

One of her friends told her about a Japanese tradition that said that anyone who folded one thousand cranes will have any wish granted by the gods. The crane is a special bird for the Japanese. It is a sign of long life and happiness.

Determined, Sadako decided that she was going to fold a thousand of these cranes. Others offered to help but she wanted to do them all. To start with Sadako folded them quickly. She sometimes wrote messages on them. As the illness made her more and more unwell she found it harder to fold the paper, but still she persevered. It must have been difficult for her family and friends to see her suffering but it must also have made them feel proud of her strength of character.

As she grew weaker she slept a lot and needed treatment, but that did not stop her trying to fold the cranes, 200, 400, 500, 600, she carried on folding aiming for a thousand.

As she became more ill the folding got slower and slower: 620, 630, 640, 642, 643 then 644. On 25th October 1955 Sadako fell asleep… and did not wake up again.

Although her friends were sad, they wanted the memory of Sadako and her bravery to live on forever. They folded the other 356 cranes themselves to make a thousand and they were buried with Sadako. They also raised money for a statue to be built in memory of all the children who had died in Hiroshima. This large statue still stands in Hiroshima's Peace Park. At the top of the statue is Sadako holding a golden folded paper crane.

Every year children from all over the world fold paper cranes and send them to her statue.

Follow-up questions
Sadako's friends were always there for her.

◆ What would you ask Sadako's best friend if you could?
◆ Do you think it is a sad story?

Brilliant Stories for Assemblies
© Paul Urry

Jack and George
(20th century)

It was 1916, two years into the first World War. Two men behind the desk glanced suspiciously at the boys then looked back down at their forms.

'How old?' one asked quietly.

'Um . . . 18,' they both lied.

Each was given a form, which they silently filled in and returned to the men behind the desk.

'Meet here next week ready for training,' they were told.

The boys nodded and left the hall. They were going to fight in the war!

The week past quickly. They learned to fire a rifle, use a bayonet, and put on gas masks. Most of all they enjoyed wearing their uniforms and being with the other young soldiers.

'Soldiers!' shouted the officer in charge. The group gathered round. 'We are off to France tomorrow, get packed up.'

Jack and George looked at each other with knots of excitement in their stomachs and smiled. *This is it.*

Conversation was buzzing on the train with the anticipation of the glory of war, the chance to defend their country.

They boarded the boat to France and travelled to the battlefield. They expected shouting, noise and guns when they arrived. Instead they heard people talking and saw huge fields with a few farm buildings. It was so different from home.

They followed an older soldier, Fred, across the field and down a ladder. They were in a trench.

As he took the final step off the ladder and stood on the wooden boarding, Jack looked at his smart, clean uniform and especially his gleaming boots. The mud had oozed up and covered the base of them. His eyes met George's.

'Oh, you'll get used to that,' said Fred. 'Follow me.'

Bending low, all three entered the small door to the wooden shelter. Gradually their eyes got used to how much darker it was. George could make out bunk beds in one corner and a small wooden table in the other.

'It's all you need,' said Fred, 'and it is safe from the bombs.'

George looked at Jack. This was not what they had expected.

As they settled in, they enjoyed the company of the other soldiers. One of their main duties was being on guard; they would stand in the trench, holding their rifles, watching out for an attack.

Most days nothing happened. Walking through the trench one day, Jack saw George. 'What are you doing?' he asked.

'Trying to write a letter to my mum. I lied to her. I said that I was not going to go to war. It is so difficult to say how I feel. I'm going to put one of these flowers in.'

(continued on next page)

Brilliant Stories for Assemblies
© Paul Urry

This page may be photocopied by the purchasing institution only.

91

George showed Jack a red flower. 'There are lots of these flowers here,' George said. 'I want my mum to imagine that I am in a nice place.'

'I know what you mean,' Jack said quietly. 'Can I have a look at the letter?'

'Sure,' George said, handing the letter and poppy to Jack to read.

As Jack started to read, shouts came from all around the trench.

'Shells overhead!' screamed their comrades. 'Get to a shelter.'

George and Jack looked at each other.

A massive explosion was heard near them. The friends ducked down. Huge amounts of mud and soil were thrown into the sky, landing on both young men. Poisonous gas filled the air. The enemy were attacking.

They fumbled around putting on their gas masks and ran as quickly as they could through the winding trenches with the other soldiers. Jack pushed past other friends and finally, heart pounding, entered a crowded shelter, exhausted.

Jack looked around the shelter. Where he had seen smiling friends before he now saw panicked faces. He saw older men holding back tears. All the time explosions could be heard outside the shelter.

The noise was deafening. Men covered their ears and tightly closed their eyes. There was nothing they could do except wait.

(continued on next page)

Brilliant Stories for Assemblies
© Paul Urry

The bombing continued all day and all night. Jack saw men asleep on their feet. For the first time in his life Jack felt completely terrified and helpless. He looked around the shelter for George.

He was not there.

Despite the constant noise of the shells, Jack eventually fell asleep, drained, leaning against another solider.

He was woken by people moving. He listened and heard nothing – the shelling had stopped There was a painful ringing in his ears. He left the shelter with the other soldiers and went to find where George was.

'Jack,' a voice called out. Jack spun round. It was Fred.

Fred walked up to him and put his hand on his shoulder. 'I'm sorry, Jack.'

Jack looked into Fred's eyes and then understood.

'We have lost a lot of soldiers in the attack. George was hit by shrapnel as he ran through the trenches. It would have been quick.'

Jack bowed his head and began to cry. As he looked down, he realized that he still had in his hand, after all the events of the last day, the piece of crumpled paper of George's letter home.

Later that day, Jack stood with the other soldiers looking at the rows and rows of graves. After the service the soldiers went back to the trench to carry on the war.

Jack was involved in many battles. He saw and did things so terrible that he never told anyone. He was not proud of what he did. He did not cheer when, several months later, he heard that the enemy had surrendered. He simply packed his bags and waited to return to his family.

On arriving back home he stopped at George's parents' house. He knocked gently at the door and waited.

They invited him in. They asked him lots of questions about George. Jack smiled and gave them George's letter. A red flower fell out.

George's mother began to cry. His father thanked him. Jack couldn't say anything.

Follow-up question

◆ Why do people wear poppies in November?

Brilliant Stories for Assemblies
© Paul Urry

This page may be photocopied by the purchasing institution only.

93

Useful websites

Cultural stories

How people got fire (North America)
            page 5
http://www.enchantedlearning.com/coloring/
Useful pictures and info about animals
http://mytwobeadsworth.com/NLoreopen.html
More native American stories

The Greedy Fishermen (Australia) **page 6**
http://www.didjshop.com/stories/index.php More
aboriginal stories

Beddgelert (Wales)   **page 7**
http://www.limaed.flyer.co.uk/wales/mountain/
gellert.html A picture of the grave
http://westwales.co.uk/graphics/gelerts_grave.jpg
The gravestone by the tree

The Bear in the Quicksand (Ancient Greece)
            page 8
http://www.mcwdn.org/fables/fabindex.html More
fables

How the kingfisher got its feathers (Africa)
            page 9
http://www.homepages.hetnet.nl/~nbhogeveen/
Vogels/Kingfishers.htm
Kingfishers from around the world

Grandpa and the wave (Japan) **pages 10–11**
http://www.atsb-malaysia.com.my/galery/Archive.
asp Large world political map

Peter and the wolf (Russia)   **page 12**
http://www.dsokids.com/2001instrumentchart.htm
Pictures of instruments used

Robert the Bruce (Scotland)   **page 13**
http://www.heritage.me.uk/people/bruce.htm
Information and pictures

The Caliph, the Beggar and the Judge (Iraq)
            page 14
http://www.atsb-malaysia.com.my/galery/Archive.
asp Large world political map

**George Washington and the Cherry Tree
(USA)**   **page 15**
http://www.frick.org/html/pntg61df.htm Painting
of George Washington

The king of the birds (Southern Africa)
          pages 16–17
http://www.ronausting.com/newpage1.htm
Pictures of birds

Greyfriars Bobby (Scotland)   **page 19**
http://ourworld.compuserve.com/homepages/
lennich/bobby.htm Photograph of bobby
http://www.picturesofedinburgh.com/pictures/
oldtown/oldtown-bobby.jpg The statue

Johnny Appleseed (USA)   **page 20**
http://www.ohiohistorycentral.org/ohc/history/es/
pic/appleseedj.shtml Drawing of Johnny
http://www.50states.com/us.htm Map of the
states of the USA

How the Years Were Named (China)
            page 21
http://www.blss.portsmouth.sch.uk/hsc/cny/cny.
shtml Masks, calendars, info

Anansi and Tiger (Jamaica) **pages 22–23**
http://www.jamaicans.com/culture/anansi/ Some
more Anansi stories and info

Religious stories

Palm Sunday   **page 28**
http://members.aol.com/Wisdomwayisraelmap.htm
Map showing the main places

St. George   **pages 29–30**
http://alabamamaps.ua.edu/world/europemed4c.jpg
Map of the Mediterranean

Lightning Source UK Ltd.
Milton Keynes UK
UKHW05f0433090418
320729UK00003B/10/P